A LONGING

TO

BELONG

A LONGING
TO
BELONG

REFLECTIONS ON
FAITH, IDENTITY, AND RACE

MICHELLE LEE-BARNEWALL

ZONDERVAN
REFLECTIVE

ZONDERVAN REFLECTIVE

A Longing to Belong
Copyright © 2023 by Michelle Lee Barnewall

Requests for information should be addressed to:
Zondervan, *3900 Sparks Dr. SE, Grand Rapids, Michigan 49546*

Zondervan titles may be purchased in bulk for educational, business, fundraising, or sales promotional use. For information, please email SpecialMarkets@Zondervan.com.

ISBN 978-0-310-12400-9 (audio)

Library of Congress Cataloging-in-Publication Data

Names: Lee-Barnewall, Michelle, 1966- author.
Title: A longing to belong : reflections on faith, identity, and race / Michelle
    Lee-Barnewall.
Description: Grand Rapids : Zondervan, 2023.
Identifiers: LCCN 2023013003 (print) | LCCN 2023013004 (ebook) | ISBN
    9780310123989 (paperback) | ISBN 9780310123996 (epub)
Subjects: LCSH: Asian American Christians. | Asian Americans--Religion. | Asian
    American women. | Korean Americans--Religion. | Race discrimination--
    Religious aspects--Christianity. | BISAC: RELIGION / Christian Living / Social
    Issues | RELIGION / Christian Theology / Ecclesiology
Classification: LCC BR563.A82 L433 2023 (print) | LCC BR563.A82 (ebook) | DDC
    230.089/95073--dc23/eng/20230517
LC record available at https://lccn.loc.gov/2023013003
LC ebook record available at https://lccn.loc.gov/2023013004

Cover design: Studio Gearbox
Cover image: © Denis Belitsky / Shutterstock
Interior design: Denise Froehlich

Printed in the United States of America

---

23 24 25 26 27 28 29 30 31 32 /TRM/ 15 14 13 12 11 10 9 8 7 6 5 4 3 2 1

To Marie

CONTENTS

INTRODUCTION

This is not a book about justice.

Although calls for justice or critiques of social justice dominate the discussion about race among Christians today, there are many people who are much better equipped to engage in that debate than I am. My offering is more personal and reflective. It is also unplanned, at least in terms of what I envisioned I would write about when I first started my career as a biblical scholar. It was not my intention to get involved in the "racial discussion." But since I have experienced a small slice of what it is like to live as a racial minority in America, I cannot help but think about how my experience fits with the worldview I have gleaned from Scripture.

Professionally, my studies have focused on the church. This too was not intentional, as it was primarily the product of finding a conundrum in Paul's letters that I thought would make an interesting dissertation topic. My exploration of the body of Christ in 1 Corinthians 12 would implant a permanent lens through which I couldn't stop thinking about what Paul and the other New Testament writers thought about unity, including racial unity.

As a result, this book represents my attempt to understand and integrate what I experienced as a child and then as an adult. I am now able to look back on those events and into the present and future through that lens. This book is intensely personal, for I believe that reconciliation must be intensely personal. Reconciliation is about how we were created to be with one another, as wondrous and unique people called to live together despite all our weaknesses and limitations, and how we are empowered by the Spirit as fellow recipients of our undeserved salvation in Christ to dwell together on this earth in truth and grace.

In other words, we were made to *belong*, and in Christ we are learning how we belong to one another and what that means. Most importantly, though, we belong to God, as his creation and as his children. This provides the foundation for all that we do.

Our belonging places certain responsibilities upon us—namely, we see ourselves and others in a new light, so that wherever we find ourselves, we may be bearers of God's life-giving grace to one another through the mercy he has shown each of us.

PART 1

CREATED TO BELONG

And if the ear should say,
"Because I am not an eye, I
do not belong to the body," it
would not for that reason stop
being part of the body. . . . But
in fact God has placed the parts
in the body, every one of them,
just as he wanted them to be.

—1 CORINTHIANS 12:16, 18

CHAPTER 1

BEGINNINGS

Of all my early childhood memories, one stands out. I was in second grade, and I had just found out from my school that the test results indicated I needed glasses. That was a time when glasses were not cool, and simply wearing them sentenced you to the farthest corner of the cafeteria with the other losers. For many kids of my era, this would be a moment of distress, weeping, and gnashing of teeth for being officially consigned to "four-eyes" status.

My reaction, though, was the opposite. I was ecstatic. I started dancing around the house, barely able to contain my excitement (and for those who know me and my generally reserved nature, the thought of my dancing in excitement is likely unbelievable enough on its own). The reason I was so happy was because in my eight-year-old mind I thought, *Now I will be able to hide my eyes! People won't be able to see that I have these small, slanty eyes, and they will stop making fun of me.*

Needless to say, I was proven wrong. I was stuck with both my eyes and my glasses. But I've always wondered about that event. I can't remember most of the incidents that prompted my misplaced victory dance, but I do recall thinking that my day of salvation had arrived because now I would be able to be like everyone else. My hopes were soon dashed, but as I grew up, I never stopped wishing that things would change, and I never stopped trying to fit in.

I grew up in a mining community in northern Minnesota, a verdant land of pine trees and lakes. Pretty much everyone owned a cabin on one of Minnesota's famous 10,000 lakes and spent their summers swimming and fishing and winters driving their snowmobiles. It was the kind of place where people bragged about being the "ice-box of the nation" every time the TV news announced that our thirty below temperature made us the coldest spot in the country, where the heroes were the local boys who played on the hockey team (especially when they beat the stuck-up rich kids from the cities down south), and where the most anticipated day of the year was the opening of hunting season.

The town was populated with Scandinavians and other European descendants, as well as their foods. We all loved pasties, handheld pastry pies made with lard and stuffed with meat and potatoes, which were significant as being the traditional food the miners took with them to work because they were filling and portable. At weddings we eagerly anticipated eating potica, a thinly rolled pastry spread with nuts, butter, cinnamon, and honey. A potica is what it would look like if a cinnamon roll and baklava had a baby in the shape of a squat bread loaf. And then there was lutefisk, whitefish pickled in lye, which no one ever admitted actually liking.

The mines were a particular source of pride, with their rich iron ore playing a critical role in supplying the American military effort in World War II. When you first entered the town limits, you were greeted with a billboard welcoming you to the "Home of the World's Largest Open Pit Iron Ore Mine," a claim to fame that lasted until a larger one was discovered in Russia, or so I was told. Even our high school yearbook was the *Hematite*, named after the highest grade of ore. On a more mundane level, my sister Marie and I liked to sit on the curb in front of our house trolling magnets in the sand so we could collect powdery iron ore filings. We spent countless afternoons engrossed in our task, getting more ore dust on our clothes than in our little baggies. We thoroughly enjoyed our pastime until one day we discovered that small souvenir bags of the stuff were sold for a dollar at the local museum.

I learned a lot in that town: No, your hair does not break off when you walk home in below zero weather with a wet head after seventh-period swimming and scrunch your frozen clumps of hair. And pizza is best sliced into small squares, as our favorite pizza shop did, since this enables you to have a single round sausage piece neatly in the center of each square. I also learned that being

Asian really, really made you stand out in a land of White, European descendants—and not in a good way.

I interpreted my experience as a statement of who I was, and what I was worth . . . or not worth. In particular, names and words were weapons used against me. Perhaps they made the name-caller feel powerful, but they made me believe I was fatally flawed. I often felt surrounded with no way to get out, never knowing when the next taunt would come. I learned early on that other people could impact me. We were created to be in community, and your community makes a difference, for better or worse.

I didn't think about all of this consciously, yet I was living out how God has made us. No other part of God's creation was formed to be in relationship with the Creator and with each other quite like humanity was. Genesis describes how God has given us each other. It was not good for man to be alone, but man and woman together were to be very good. We were created for community, but the reality of the fall means that our greatest wounds too often come from those we are in community with.

Of course, I am not alone in being impacted by others. It is easy to see that we affect one another. A harsh word can be devastating, but an encouraging word from a teacher can turn someone's life around, like it did for my husband. Scripture repeatedly warns us to consider who we associate with. We can see our character suffer by keeping bad company (1 Cor. 15:33), or we can sharpen one another like iron (Prov. 27:17). We are to "walk with the wise and become wise, for a companion of fools suffers harm" (13:20). The author of Hebrews tells us to "spur one another on toward love and good deeds" (10:24). The disciples provide a great example of this, as they learned from living and journeying with Jesus.

As I tried to figure out my place in the world, I was shaped by my encounters with others. There were many positive events, while some of the hurtful ones continue to surprise me with their persistence and depth. The good news of the gospel includes the truth that despite our human limitations, frailties, and insecurities, through Christ we can give grace and life to others. The bad news of the fall is that sin too often mars our ability or inclination to be that good for one another, and we inflict damage instead. Growing up, I encountered the harm that comes from that sin.

From kindergarten to my senior year in high school, I was the only Asian kid in my class. By the time I graduated, my class of over 300 also had three Black kids, and they were the only other students who were singled out because of their race. My high school had some Native Americans (this being northern Minnesota, after all), but they didn't stand out by their race as much as their socioeconomic status. For the most part, they were part of the group who were uncharitably labeled the "burn-outs," who regularly skipped class to smoke in back of the high school and weren't expected to go to college.

Not surprisingly, being different was a defining feature of my childhood, and wanting to be like everyone else—to be "normal"—was my never-ending and never-achieved childhood goal. Being different made me believe there was something wrong with me. People made fun of those who were different: if you were the poorest or most awkward kid in class, if you were always playing the wrong note in band, or if you were the only boy whose dad made you get a crew cut, which was not in style in the early '70s. I wanted to be normal because being normal meant you were okay. Conversely, if you weren't normal, you weren't okay. And if you're a kid, you really want to be okay.

I grew up equating White with normal, which meant that not being White was *not normal*. You weren't so different that you weren't part of the human race, but you were just different enough to be the wrong kind of human, a little less than others. In that environment, being Korean was definitely different.

All this made me especially anxious about going to new places where people didn't know me. One summer, I let a friend persuade me to go to summer camp with her. I didn't want to go, but she didn't want to go alone, so I reluctantly agreed. I think I was around nine or ten years old, one of those ages when you are taking serious steps to forming your identity and acutely aware of what other people think about you. As soon as we got to the camp, she ran into some older (i.e., cooler) friends of hers, and I was promptly dumped. I was pretty upset about it, although the situation was somewhat mitigated because

I became friends with a sweet and delightful girl, with whom I hung around for the rest of the week. Brooke was very petite and endearing, with an inviting and sincere smile and a kind and innocent spirit. She also had long, silky, blond hair, which she tied loosely in pigtails on the sides of her head so that they covered her ears, and which I envied with all of my heart.

As much as I enjoyed my time with Brooke, I spent a fair amount of the week dreading the big dance that was the much-anticipated climax of the camp session. I had already endured a number of "chink" comments and slanty-eyed faces, and so I knew what fate awaited me. I can't remember what I dreaded most—being rejected, or the public humiliation of people seeing and knowing I was rejected.

Perhaps I made my own self-fulfilling prophecy, but as it turns out, I was right on the mark. We all sat in a big circle in full view of one another, and I watched all of the other girls get asked to dance, including the girl all the other girls hated (except Brooke, of course, who liked everyone) and who would have been voted "most obnoxious" had they given that prize. I watched happy girl after happy girl get asked to dance by the boy or boys she had her eyes on, while I remained seated in my chair waiting for what I knew would not come.

Or at least not come in the way I wanted. Some sixth graders, the top of the elementary school hierarchy, apparently felt sorry for me. One of them made her younger brother ask me to dance, *made* being the operative word. When he asked me, the look on his face made clear what he really thought about the situation. My inner warning bell signaled that I would be better off politely saying no, but something else inside me couldn't resist. I jumped up and said yes. Despite the fact that I knew his asking voluntarily was an illusion, I was overcome by my preadolescent girl's longing to be led onto the dance floor by a cute boy and the thrill of seeming to be "chosen." As we walked onto the spotlighted floor, for a brief moment I no longer felt rejected and instead could believe I was normal and that everyone could see it.

I should have listened to my instincts. The boy had asked me to a slow dance, one of those things that eternally symbolize affirmation for insecure preadolescent girls all over America. However, to say he did not relish the idea of being with me would be an understatement. His facial expression suggested he would rather have his eyes pecked out by crows. As we "danced," he kept me as far away from him as humanly possible while still maintaining some kind of contact. This was clearly not enough to satisfy his older sister. She and her friends started shouting for him to hold me closer, to which he responded to them with a loud and annoyed growl, "I know, I know!"

I'm not sure which was more humiliating to my fourth-grade self: having to have someone force her little brother to dance with me, knowing everyone else knew she had to force her little brother to dance with me, or enduring the distinct look of disgust on his face for the odious task he was forced to perform. So while I got my dance, it was at great cost, as the public humiliation only added to my sense of shame.

Needless to say, I felt terrible about the whole evening. The next morning Brooke noticed I was down and asked me if it was because of what had happened the previous night. Her question came out of genuine caring, but having her verbalize it only confirmed my public rejection. Acknowledging it somehow made my shame feel even more real and unbearable. To avoid that pain, I just said I was upset with my friend who had abandoned me, which was not untrue.

⌇

All week at the camp, I tried so hard to fit in, only to fail miserably in the end. Some good things had happened, meeting Brooke in particular, but I left with an even more penetrating and permanent sense of rejection, of being excluded for something I could not change.

When I reflect on what happened and how I reacted, I can't help but wonder: Why do we crave to fit in? Why do we need to belong?

As a child I was driven by that need. But I shouldn't be surprised. Scripture makes clear from the beginning that we were meant be a part of something other than ourselves, and that something includes other people. Eve was created so Adam would not be alone.

To be part of a community is to be accepted by others, to participate in something bigger than yourself, to not be alone. It is, as one author writes, "one of the fundamental longings of our lives."[1]

This is something we see throughout Scripture. As an evangelical, I am used to thinking about myself as an individual. After all, I made a "personal" decision for Christ, who loved me so much that he died for me. I am told to contribute to the church through my particular ministry. I am urged to identify my specific sins so the Holy Spirit can help me overcome those temptations.

As true as that may be, all that emphasis on *me* often causes me to miss the *we*. And I don't mean *we* as in "we all need to do our part" or even "we all need to get along." What I'm talking about is the *we* that exists as a people, a group, a whole with its own identity, of which I am a part, and how understanding and living in that identity matters.

In 1 Corinthians 12 we see how we can miss this corporate aspect and how that can make a difference. This well-known passage is often used to emphasize that every member in the body of Christ has something to contribute through their spiritual gifts, and that each contribution is important. This understanding usually leads to a couple of different responses. The first is teaching that everyone should identify their spiritual gift, and then use it. Furthermore, everyone should value their gift and not feel bad if their gift does not seem as "important" as others. We should not envy the talented singers and musicians who are up on stage every Sunday because we are just as needed if our gift is setting up the chairs for the Sunday service or being able to get the right donuts for the after-service fellowship time.

While these are noble goals, and to a large extent I agree with them, there are also some critical elements that are being overlooked. I have a friend who has written a book describing how the emphasis on searching for our "gift" can be problematic. It can cause us to limit our ministry to what we think our "gift" is rather than stepping out in faith in whatever situation we might find ourselves and trusting God to provide his Spirit to help us accomplish his will in that situation.[2]

Another problem I see with the typical interpretation of the passage is that Paul is not talking about *doing* at all. The passage is about *being* who we are.

This distinction is important, for it underscores something crucial in Paul's thought. Americans are a pragmatic people. We like to *do* things. So it is not surprising we approach 1 Corinthians 12 in this way.

But we miss a lot if we fail to see Paul's focus on who we are. Just as my behavior as an individual flows out of what I believe about myself, so too are our actions as a community influenced by how we see ourselves as a whole. We can't skip the step of seeing the body of Christ as our identity because who we are corporately is as much a part of our identity as who we are in Christ individually. This corporate lens is vital for how we ought to think of ourselves and everyone else.

For those who are data driven (or grammar geeks like me), it might be helpful to know that there are no imperatives, or commands, in 1 Corinthians 12 until verse 31.[3] However, in 1 Corinthians 14, where Paul continues the discussion of spiritual gifts, he uses over twenty imperatives, such as in verse 12: "Since you are eager for gifts of the Spirit, try to excel in those that build up the church." That's an important difference in emphasis. We miss what Paul is saying to us if we overlook his focus on *being* more than *doing* in chapter 12.

Consider how in 12:15, Paul says, "If the foot should say, 'Because I am not a hand, I do not belong to the body,' it would not for that reason stop being part of the body.'" Paul is not telling the foot to quit saying it doesn't belong. Rather, he's saying that even *if* the foot does say that, it is still a member of the body. The foot doesn't stop belonging to the body just because it doesn't feel like it and is lamenting. Being a member of the body is its identity. It's not a choice; it's a truth.

Or take verse 21, "The eye cannot say to the hand, 'I don't need you!'" Paul is not telling the eye to stop saying that to the hand. Instead, Paul is claiming that the eye cannot rightly say that to the hand because the eye truly needs the hand, even if the eye doesn't believe it. Paul continues: "On the contrary, those parts of the body that seem to be weaker are indispensable" (v. 22). If the eye feels superior, it is only demonstrating how little it knows about the nature and worth of the hand.

Why might this matter? Paul is not telling the body parts who think they have an inferior gift to quit feeling inferior. He is not saying, "Stop doing this!" Instead, he is telling them they are members of the body just like everyone else. In other words, "This is who you are!" He is not telling the superior-feeling parts that they shouldn't say they don't need others. Rather, he is telling them that they can't say it because all the parts are valuable. Paul wants to correct them by first clarifying how they should think about themselves and others based on the truth of their new existence in Christ.

Paul knows that how we identify ourselves and others matters. He brings his instruction to a head in verse 27 with a straightforward declaration of their identity, "Now you are the body of Christ, and each one of you is a part of it." For Paul, belonging is the beginning.

We don't need Paul to tell us that people want to be a part of something bigger. This is evident even in young children. We see it in the groups they form on the playground, and we feel deeply for the child who is left out. We know intuitively that we were created to connect. But what happens when we feel excluded from the group? Or even worse, what happens when we are made explicitly aware that we don't fit in, that we are the only one who isn't a member of the group, and that everyone else knows it? We were created to belong, and we will do anything to make it happen.

CHAPTER 2

NOT FITTING IN

I learned a particularly vivid lesson about not fitting in one day on the elementary school playground. One of my classmates ran up to me with a sense of urgency, grabbing me by the arm and pulling me toward a crowd of kids huddled around something. I wondered why I was summoned with such seriousness. My heart jumped as I interpreted this need for me as proof that I was one of them. I felt a flicker of significance.

As I was ushered into the circle, my momentary uplift of childish hope turned into a sinking heart. Recently, a family of Vietnamese refugees had been resettled in the community. One of the younger kids from that family was crying unconsolably (and being surrounded by a big group of older kids seemed to make him even more inconsolable, although no one picked up on that). I was needed because the little boy only spoke Vietnamese, so no one could understand why he was upset. Their solution? See if I could talk with him.

I don't harbor any hard feelings against my classmates, since it was clear from the looks on their faces that they meant no harm. They were just trying to fix the situation before the teachers arrived because they were worried they would get in trouble. I can see how it made sense in their elementary school minds that someone who kind of looked like the crying boy might be able to talk to him.

For me, the incident was profoundly revealing and demoralizing. It solidified my sense of differentness. Growing up, there were moments when I was under the blissful illusion that maybe I did fit and my classmates didn't see me as different. But this incident disclosed the truth. Just as moments of stress show people's true character, as they act out of instinct, emergencies also expose how people really see you. Even if I felt accepted and protected by my closest friends, most of my classmates—who constituted a big part of my world—saw me as different, more like the Vietnamese refugee kids who couldn't speak English than like someone who had grown up in America just like them. I spoke the same language, saw the same movies, played the same schoolyard games, read the same books, and ate the same foods, yet I could never escape what I looked like, no matter who I was on the inside.

Harvard philosophy professor Charles Taylor states, "One is a self only among other selves. A self can never be described without reference to those who surround it."[1] A critical aspect of our identity is formed in community, in relationship with others. As a child, this was how I learned my identity.

My relationship with the world was inescapable, and the sense of not fitting in was pervasive. There was nowhere I could go in town where I felt like I was just like everyone else. I was constantly reminded of my status by the usual Asian slurs (chink, Chinaman, gook, Jap), sound effects (gongs, high-pitched tones, and other musical effects), gestures (fingers drawing back slanted eyes), or a combination of these (the ubiquitous "Ah so" with accompanying mocking bow). I became so sensitive to being mocked that I would involuntarily recoil when I heard the otherwise benign phrase "a chink in the armor."

I came to believe there was something necessary to be a real member of the community, and that something was being White. I also discovered that lived experience is very hard to counteract, especially when you're only beginning to learn about the world and your place in it, and you have no other reference points.

I experienced a sense of hopelessness, that there was nothing I could do to feel accepted—like getting a new haircut, or a nice blouse, or glasses. This became clear to me through one of my last attempts in high school to be "normal." I became a majorette in the marching band. There were several reasons I thought this was great. I was able to ditch my flute and get out of the mass of instrument players, who always had to march in packed, straight lines, which I couldn't do well and for which I was continually being yelled at by the upperclassmen. Even better, the majorettes got to wear their uniforms to school on game days. I thought being able to prance around the high school halls in my little baton-twirler outfit on the day of the big football game would show I was "cool," like being a cheerleader.

In becoming a majorette, I believed I had finally accomplished something that would grant me full acceptance so I could be like everyone else. But that illusion was shattered the day I stood outside my house with my friend Debbie, holding my supposedly cool majorette baton while two little kids on bicycles pedaled by, laughing as they sang those all-too-familiar ching-chong-Chinaman chants. Debbie was supportive and sympathetic, calling them jerks, but my high hopes for acceptance were devastated by the taunts of those little kids. "What do I have to do to fit in?" I thought. But I already knew the answer. I can't *do* anything.

※

While I can appreciate the intention behind the popular children's saying "Sticks and stones may break my bones, but names will never hurt me," it's clear that whoever came up with that ditty didn't get it from the Bible. Yes, it's intended to help children withstand name calling and other insults and teach them there are ways to stand up against bullies rather than getting even. Certainly, there is some truth to the idea that words are just things people say. Their words aren't necessarily true, and we don't have to accept them.

But names can also be very powerful, for they reflect how others see us. And it is hard to resist the power of someone else's assessment when you don't know who you are. That was my experience growing up. Since I had zero understanding of what it meant to be "in Christ" at that time, I had no defense against their words and nowhere to hide from their cutting evaluations of who I was.

What's in a name? A lot, actually.

When names are given by someone who wants good for us, they can be life-giving. When names are given by someone who wishes us ill, they can be devastating. Names can be characterizations. They can inspire us to live up to them (gifted, kind-hearted, hero). Others are wholly negative, and we try with all our might to free ourselves from their power (klutz, stupid, ugly). Names can be used to express a special relationship (sweetheart, honey, BFF), or they can be used to wound and isolate (loser, chicken, freak).

The Scriptures reflect the ancient significance of naming, and we see this right from the beginning in the creation of the world. God begins with the ordering and *naming* of the world. He creates light and calls the light "day" and the darkness "night." After he forms the earth, he names the sky, the land, and the seas (Gen. 1:5–10). After making animals and birds, he creates the man, who names the creatures, and then the man names the woman God creates for him (Gen. 2:19–23; 3:20).

Names identify. In the older way of thinking, they reflected a person's character or perhaps their role or destiny.[2] A name might have described the essence of who a person was. To know someone's name was to know their nature.[3]

Adam names the woman Eve "because she would

become the mother of all the living" (Gen. 3:20). In Genesis 17:5, God renames Abram as Abraham to signify that he will be the father of many nations. Jacob becomes Israel because he struggled with God and prevailed (Gen. 32:28). When Simon declares Jesus as the Christ, he is renamed Peter because of the significance of his declaration (Matt. 16:17–18).

Names can also reflect lineage. We see this in the names that begin with *Bar*, which means "son of." We have Bar-Timaeus (Mark 10:46), Bar-Jesus (Acts 13:6), Bar-Jonah (Matt. 16:17; John 1:42; 21:15), and even Bar-Abbas (Matt. 27:15–26; John 18:40)![4]

Names can even reveal the character of God. *El Shaddai* means "God Almighty" (Gen. 17:1), *El Elyon* is "God Most High," referring to God as the master of creation (Gen. 14:18–20). *Yahweh Shammah* is "THE LORD IS THERE" (Ezek. 48:35).[5] The infant Jesus is called *Immanuel*, which means "God with us" (Matt.1:23).

The list goes on.

We should not so quickly dismiss the importance of names. We know intuitively that names are significant, that they are markers for a person. Why else do we admire, scoff, or shake our heads at what parents name their children? Why does it hurt us so much when we are called clumsy, fat, or an idiot?

Racial slurs are no different. They tell the recipient that they are less than, undesirable, and "other." They exclude someone from a community, propping up one's own sense of identity at the other's expense. To be on the receiving end of a slur is to feel the other person's condescension, disdain, or hatred. When I was a kid trying really, really hard to be like everyone else, I learned that names have a tremendous ability to build up or tear down—and through them we wield enormous power to do good or do harm.

$$\overline{\overline{}}\!\!\!\diagdown\!\!\!\diagup\!\!\!\diagdown$$

The names we accept as true can be powerful signs for how we think about ourselves. A single name can convey a world of ideas, images, and emotions. Names define our identity.

And identity matters.

We often have many names and many identities, or perhaps many parts to our identity. I may have an overarching identity in Christ, but my specific life in this world requires a number of additional identities within and beyond that, some of which I carry more strongly than others at any particular time. For instance, I am a professor, but when I am with my grandchildren, being a professor is irrelevant. Instead, I am Halmoni, which is Korean for "grandmother" (and for my three-year-old granddaughter, more properly stated, "Homie"). I am both a wife and a daughter, and at various points I am recognized more as one than the other. I am also a dog-lover, a mediocre cook, a slow reader, and someone who colors her hair even though I swore in my twenties I would never be so vain.

It's not that I wanted to focus on being Asian in any unique way when I was growing up. Just the opposite! But being Asian became an inescapable part of my existence when it was continually pointed out to me as the primary way in which I was not like everyone else. Needless to say, it caused all sorts of problems and confusion as I tried to understand who I was.

When you don't fit in, and especially when you're the only one who isn't like everyone else, you don't just feel inferior—you feel like you're a misfit, a freak. When I look back at my childhood, I now see how much my world and my thoughts revolved around trying to be like everyone else and how hard I tried to convince myself that I was. I was desperate for and determined to change my identity, even if I didn't consciously think about it in those specific terms.

Everyone in northern Minnesota ice skates. So like many other parents, my mother signed my sister and me up for lessons. On those dark, cold winter mornings when we were in elementary school, she would drag us over to the ice rink to get in some skating practice before school. I'm not sure why she did it. Neither my sister nor I were enthusiastic about the sport, nor did we show any real potential. However, there we were with all the other kids, day after day, lacing up our skates beforehand and complaining about our frozen feet afterward.

Because enough parents were willing to subject their disinterested and sleep-deprived kids to this morning torture, the town put on an ice show every year. This was an opportunity to showcase the local talent—that is, the few kids who could actually perform while the rest of us in our sequined tutus and pink bunny outfits just tried to make it to the end of the rink without falling down.

Not surprisingly, most of us didn't take it very seriously. We were a bunch of goof-offs, with only Kate H. able to do anything halfway decent (she could land a single axel!). But then, one year, our instructor was a former Olympic skater from South Korea. How she ended up in our town, I don't recall, but nevertheless, there she was, trying to persuade us that if we just worked harder, we could make it to the big leagues.

At my first and only private lesson with the Olympian,

she decided that the problem with my jumps was that I was way too slow. If I could get more speed going into the jump, it would give me the force necessary to complete the requisite twirls and start me on the road to skating greatness. So she took it upon herself to show me how this worked. Grabbing me by the hand, she began pulling me around the rink so I could experience that level of speed—and consequently, a successful jump—firsthand.

Now, figure skating seems very different when you have a bird's eye view of the tiny ice princesses bopping around on TV rather than when you are actually *on* the ice. Olympic figure skaters are *really fast* and going that fast can be *really scary*. She proceeded to whip me around the ice at lightning speed, skating backward no less. The icy air cut across my face while I saw the bleachers whiz by in a blur. I was trying my best not to cry as I had visions of crashing into the sideboards head first at ninety miles an hour.

The instructor, of course, thought this was exactly what I needed. And as we reached the other end of the rink, she yelled, "Jump!" Meanwhile I am thinking, "Are you *crazy*, lady?" After she yelled at me again, I decided I had to do something. I screeched to a halt, tentatively stuck out my leg behind me, tapped my toe pick into the ice, and produced a sad little hop. I was simply relieved to have survived a near-death experience, but the instructor was less than pleased with my lack of potential. She skated off in a huff, presumably looking for someone more willing to risk life and limb for Olympic glory.

That instructor left after less than a year. I later heard

from a neighbor that she had several complaints about the town. Despite her brief tenure, of all the instructors we had growing up, she is the only one I remember, and it is not because of our private lesson.

At the annual skating show that year, she performed a solo that wowed everyone in the crowd. As I watched her tiny figure spotlighted in the darkened ice rink, I recall thinking how odd she looked as a Korean in front of that all-White audience. As I look back now, I'm struck by how the irony of my thought completely escaped me at the time. That Korean instructor created a weird sense of disconnect for me. I could see that she looked different from everyone else because she was Asian, but I still clung to the illusion that somehow—despite being Asian myself—*I* could fit in. I had a vague sense that I could identify with her since she looked like me, but at the same time I didn't identify with her *because I saw that she didn't fit in—whereas I (at least at that time) believed I did*. To put it simply, there was an identity I wanted, and another one I rejected. And I was determined to turn the one I wanted into reality, even when it wasn't.

This may sound confusing, but it reflects my own confusion at the time. That's the funny thing about being a child (though we never really outgrow it): you can want something so badly that you will twist your understanding of reality to achieve it.

This event showed me how powerful our minds are, able to redefine reality to an extent. It also showed me how deep the need to belong is. I tried as hard as I could to convince myself I was like everyone else, whether or not it was the truth. I would eventually learn that I needed to accept the way things were. Even more importantly, I would learn that my race and ethnicity were integral to who God created me to be and also part of the challenge and promise of what it means to be a member of the one body of Christ.

CHAPTER 3

REJECTION AND GRACE

Rejection is a form of death. That's what it felt like to me. But the opposite is also true. There is something life-giving about being accepted. Perhaps it's better to say there is an acceptance that says I am willing to know you, see you, and be with you. This acceptance is a kind of grace, a grace that gives us life.

As bizarre as some of my responses to rejection seem to me now, I acted the way I did because I was trying to escape the death of rejection. Scripture tells us there is another way to escape death—through life-giving grace.

We often think of grace as God's forgiveness of our sins. That's true, and it is wonderful, astounding, and incomprehensible. But there is more to grace than accounting. God's acceptance cannot be reduced to a line in a ledger.

Grace is personal. It means I do not need to make sure I fit certain criteria to have a relationship, that I can fall short, and that there is more to me that matters than what can be seen on the outside or through my actions. Grace sees you as a person—hopeful, vulnerable, yearning. It accepts you, providing rest and safety in the openness of the relationship. And we all have an incredible privilege: we can give this grace to each other.

T he parable of the prodigal son is one of the most beloved passages in Scripture. Even people who have never cracked open a Bible know the story. We often focus on the father's forgiveness, and we should, but there is another level to the parable. It reveals the father's relationship to the son and what lies at the core of their relationship.

In the story, the son asks for his inheritance from his father. The son receives it and promptly squanders it in dissolute living. Starving and alone, he makes a desperate decision to humble himself and return to his father. He seeks only to be treated like a hired hand, as he believes that is the most he can hope for. Instead, he is given a most remarkable and unbelievable welcome. The father runs to greet his long-lost son, an action that would have been considered disgraceful and undignified for him in the ancient Near Eastern culture of that time. He orders his servants to put his "best robe" on his son, likely his own robe reserved for special occasions. And then he immediately orders a feast to be given in the son's honor. This welcome wasn't just a nice party. It was over the top. The father's reaction stands in stark contrast to the magnitude of the son's original offense against his father.[1] We do not learn the son's reaction, although we are given a sense of the shocking greatness of the father's response from his older son's reaction. The older brother complains bitterly about the celebration given in honor of his younger brother, who gravely dishonored their father.

When I think about the younger son, I imagine how he felt. I feel an enormous sense of relief knowing my days of running and hiding are over. I am able to let down my guard, having found freedom from my shame, knowing I am accepted as I am. I can rest again. I sense wonderment at my acceptance by my father, the same one I have profoundly humiliated but who now seems only concerned with bringing me back into the family. Here is a father who not only refused to reject his son but also gave life back to a crushed soul by means of his immense joy at his son's return. The father is not ignoring the grave injustice committed against him. He is focusing instead on what matters most—the son himself. The father does not condone the son's transgression but demonstrates that the son's identity *as his son* mattered more.

This is the rest that comes from grace. This is what God gives us in Jesus. It includes but is far deeper and richer than just knowing our sin is forgiven. This grace sees us as we are—incredibly imperfect and yet worthy because we were created in the image of God, because God made us with souls that think and feel, and because he gave us the capacity to love and be loved. His grace provides us with security and hope in a broken and fallen world. When we share this grace with others—God's grace—we are sharing a grace that sees and values the person.

And yet all too often, we don't do this.

The younger son in this parable thought he would be rejected because of his sin, despite his repentance and remorse. But we reject people all the time for things that have nothing to do with sin, sometimes for simply not being the person we think they should be, expect them to be, or want them to be. Sometimes we reject people simply because it makes us feel good and powerful.

Rejecting someone "just because," refusing to see them as they are, can crush their spirit. Accepting someone, being willing to see and be with them as they are, can be life-giving.

This grace says,

> You are different than me, but I want to be
>   in relationship with you.
> I may never understand why you do the
>   things you do, but I can still be in
>   relationship with you.
> I disagree with/hate your views, but I will
>   not reject you.

This grace declares that sameness, conformity, and perfection are not initial requirements for a relationship. It says that there is something far deeper, far more valuable about who we are as people that matters: that we can be with one another despite seemingly unbridgeable chasms because we know that, at its core, being human is something wonderful, mysterious, immensely valuable—something we all share.

The grace to be with one another is possible because it comes first from the Father, who says,

> You have rebelled against me,
>   mocked me,
>   hardened your heart against me,
>   caused me great pain by your callous
>   indifference to me . . .
>
> but I long to be in relationship with you.

This grace is the opposite of rejection, or scorn, or violence. It does not set us *against* one another but invites us to be *with* one another. It enables us not only to live together but to thrive together.

In Luke 7 Jesus is eating at the home of Simon the Pharisee. A woman, weeping, comes to Jesus and anoints his feet. Her gratitude, repentance, and devotion are on full display. Simon declares her a sinner, but Jesus sees her as something more. He declares she is someone who has faith, someone who is forgiven, someone who loves.

Jesus says to Simon, "Do you see this woman?" (Luke 7:44). A friend once pushed me to consider the power behind this question.[2] Do you *see* her? Perhaps Jesus means more than Simon's ability to see her with his eyes. Perhaps Jesus is inviting Simon to see her in her humanity, as someone created by God and of immeasurable worth, someone who has felt the pain of shattered dreams and the scorn of the righteous crowd. This woman is seen—by Jesus, if not Simon—and he brings her from death to life.

Scripture often revolves around the theme of rejection. Peter wants to reject the gentiles because they aren't Jews (Acts 10). The gentiles reject the Jews because they are, well, Jews. The woman at the well doesn't expect Jesus to talk with her because she is a Samaritan and a woman (John 4). The world expects God to reject sinners, as we rejected him (Rom. 5:6–8).

But God does the opposite. He dies for us.

Instead of rejecting us, Jesus invites us to be with him. His grace is what saves us and transforms us. It is life-giving, enabling us to be people who give life-giving grace to others, loving as he has loved us (John 13:34; 15:12). Since we have no option but to live with each other, every day we face a choice. How will we receive one another, despite our differences? We can choose to be those who give grace and life.

———※———

We all have an unquenchable yearning to know we have a place, to know that others care about us, to know that we matter. While our deepest healing comes from knowing that God loves us and created us in his image, we can still help by giving that gift of acceptance to each other. Although I felt fundamentally displaced in the Midwestern town of my childhood, I found the gift of gracious acceptance in my little circle of friends.

From kindergarten through high school, my closest friends were my refuge. When I was with them, I never worried about being a "chink" or a "gook." They made me feel like I was one of them—worthy of a goofy nickname, confidante of whispered secrets about our teachers, companion for the activities and events school-aged kids in our day shared. We spent Friday nights going to the movies, met each other at piano lessons, and thought going all the way to Pizza Hut at the Irongate Mall during our lunch hour was a daring outing. We were good kids who studied hard, didn't drink or party (for the most part), and in general respected adults and followed the rules.

I felt like I fit with my friends. They didn't ignore the fact I was Asian. They simply saw me as their friend, Michelle, who was Korean but even more so the person they shared band trips with, agonized with over math exams, and ate lunch with in the gym (which was the cool place). We shared life together.

Although I was too quiet to be the dominant person in our group, there were times when I was somehow seen as the representative of our little pack. When it came time to choose the president for the National Honor Society, one friend thought it would be a great idea to nominate me. The idea horrified me (or perhaps I just panicked) as I realized I had no idea whatsoever how to fulfill whatever responsibilities the position might entail, and so I begged him not to do that. Despite my objections, he believed our nerd coalition was numerous enough for one of us to win over the popular kids, and apparently the others did too. Even though I ran a passionate anticampaign, telling everyone not to vote for me because I would be the worst president ever, they didn't listen and I ended up winning by one vote over the captain of the hockey team.

Being with my friends I felt like . . . a person. From them, I learned how nice it is to be with people who accept you the way you are, loving one another even when we cannot fully relate to everything about them.

I thrived under the acceptance of my friends, but once I stepped outside their protective bubble, the wider world was not so gracious. Another incident always lurked around the corner. I never knew when I would encounter another comment, a jeering laugh, or some other reminder that I did not fit in.

The standard definition of what was normal and not normal was constantly communicated to me, along with the message that I didn't fit the standard. I concluded that the problem must be me. The rest of the world is normal and I alone am not.[3] Even though my friends might accept me, I could not move beyond what I had learned from the larger world. So it was incredibly profound when I later learned that being who I was—being *Korean*—could also be part of my identity and could be something good.

After high school, I left my small Midwestern town and headed to a big city on the East Coast to attend college. In the blink of an eye, my world grew bigger. Suddenly, I was no longer the *only* one. There were others like me!

In college I discovered that I could belong to a community where I was not the sole person who looked like me. There were other Asians in my classes and in my dorm. In particular, I had two Chinese American friends, and we bonded over our late night sessions talking about guys, making cookies, and complaining about our strict parents. At long last, I felt that sense of being normal, even being Asian.

I don't recall ever consciously acknowledging this like: "Wow, this is great. I have moved from being completely self-conscious and feeling bad about who I am to now feeling fulfilled and complete in my differentness." There was never a notable event or a mind-blowing transition, and at the time, I didn't think much about my faith or how it might impact my identity. Rather, I just felt at ease, no longer being constantly assaulted by a sense of not fitting in and having to be always vigilant to protect myself against the next threat.

I transitioned fairly seamlessly into my new environment, simply enjoying my newfound freedom without any deep thoughts about my identity. But I do remember one thing: for the first time I was comfortable being Asian. And I didn't need to be around other Asians all the time to feel this. Being Asian was now a part of me, but it didn't dominate my life. I could think about it, or not. It was okay to be Asian, with all its good aspects and bad aspects, rather than believing I had some kind of personal deformity that made me want to hide what I looked like whenever I went outside. That's what mattered to me.

In a memoir of coming to America as an impoverished, illegal Chinese immigrant, Qian Julie Wang recounts how when she moved from China to the United States, she had to accept that she was now "no longer normal."[4] In my isolation growing up, I thought I was the only one who felt that way. As I have talked with others and read other people's stories, I am amazed at how commonplace those thoughts are. Calls for justice dominate the social, religious, and political landscape today, but on a mundane day-to-day basis, I suspect a lot of people also just want to feel "normal."

Carl Trueman states, "If our identities are shaped by our connection to and interaction with significant others, then identity also arises in the context of belonging."[5]

I found one type of belonging with my high school pals, who saw beyond my being Korean. I found another kind of belonging when I learned that being Asian could be a positive part of who I was. It was possible for me to fit in as Asian. And while all this may sound a bit paradoxical, I believe it accurately reflects our complexity as human beings. We do ourselves a disservice if we pretend identity can be reduced to easy formulas or catchy slogans. As earth- and time-bound humans, our identities in Christ take their particular shape in the context of our daily lives, in all our layered and complex relationships with each other and with the world around us. We were created to be with each other, and being together is no simple task.

PART 2

BELONGING TOGETHER

Therefore, as we have opportunity,
let us do good to all people,
especially to those who belong
to the family of believers.

—GALATIANS 6:10

CHAPTER 4

A PART OF SOMETHING BIGGER

Years ago, I read a story about why we should be part of a local church. The story, often attributed to the evangelist D. L. Moody or sometimes to an anonymous pastor, goes like this:

> One cold, wintery day, a pastor went to the home of a man who had decided he did not need to go to church and instead could worship God well enough in the privacy of his home. Sitting in front of the fire, the two talked briefly. The pastor then stood up quietly, went to the fire, picked up a single piece of coal with the tongs, and set it by itself on the hearth. It was not long before the ember, which had burned so brightly when gathered with the other pieces of coal, began to smolder until finally, it went out.

When I hear this, I'm reminded that I need others. I need to gather with other believers so we can support one another. But I can't help but wonder if there is something even more fundamental than knowing what I should do. Being told what to do and following rules can be helpful, but it gets tiresome after a while. Knowing I should do something does little to change my heart or my desires. On the other hand, truly knowing who I am can have a profound impact on what I do because it changes how I look at something. It reflects what I value, what I truly want, and that influences and drives what I do.

I have read books and commentaries about what we are to do as members of the body of Christ. Many are good and helpful. For example, we are to love one another and use our gifts for the benefit of the whole. It's hard to argue with that. What I don't tend to find in those books, however, is someone telling me what it means to *be* the corporate body of Christ and the power lying behind that identity.

The idea of a new corporate identity is something that is often lost or glossed over in our quest to understand what Christ has done for us individually. But for Paul, it's essential. Our understanding of who we are as a *whole*, as a bound-together people, is just as important as our individual identities in Christ. Jesus proclaimed a radical new identity for his followers in both ways—individually and corporately. These identities are intertwined. To know who we are as individuals, we must also know who we are in the community and what that larger whole is.[1]

We *are* the body of Christ. We *are* the family of God.

Our corporate identity impacts how we understand ourselves as individuals and also how we respond to the world and each other. But what does that mean when we talk about race or have discussions about our racial and ethnic differences? Is our racial identity important anymore? If so, which is more important—the individual or the whole? Does our race matter—such as the fact that I am Asian—or does it no longer matter once I know that I am in Christ? Isn't being one in Christ the point?

When I think about the role of corporate identity in our lives, I'm reminded of my parents, who left one country to find a home in another. Their struggle was constantly about figuring out where they belonged and how they fit. Although my parents' journey was very much an individual quest in pursuit of the "American dream," their story was inevitably framed by their efforts to integrate into a community and the tension of leaving behind one group identity and searching for another. They repeatedly ran into the obstacle of trying to get their Korean family to belong as part of this new and very White country. But the larger lesson I learned from them was the importance of belonging to something bigger than yourself and knowing how and why that something-you-were-a-part-of mattered.

⎯⎯⟋⋀⟍⎯⎯

When I tell people where I grew up, a common response I get is, "How did your family end up *there?*" The emphasis on *there* reveals the real question, "How did a Korean family end up in a northern

Minnesota mining town filled with blond-haired blue-eyed Scandinavians?" or perhaps even more accurately, "What were your parents *thinking*?"

One answer is that my dad was receiving medical training at the University of Minnesota, and to avoid being deported, he needed a job to show that it was in America's interest for him to remain in the country. The local hospital was having problems filling their open position for an anesthesiologist because that person would be the only one in the region—essentially on call 24-7. My father's way of showing his valuable contribution to the country was to take a job no one else wanted.

The deeper answer is that my parents really wanted to be in America, so they did what they could to come to this country and remain here. My father would later talk about how he came to America with dreams of living in New York City but ended up in a mining town near the Canadian border, where he would live for over forty years. Life in that town was challenging, not just because of the workload but because our little family was so isolated. There were many good aspects to our time there, but in reality we were there because my parents had no other choice if they wanted to stay in America.

My parents grew up in the 1930s and '40s, living through the Japanese occupation of Korea and World War II. Both of them had wanted to come to America for a long time, seeing it as the land of opportunity. They lived in a country continually torn apart by war, foreign oppression, and limited dreams. My father's family had been very successful and educated; they were philosophers, civil servants, and teachers. My mother's family had been fairly prosperous landowners. They lost everything.

My siblings and I grew up knowing very little about our parents' lives before they came to America or even what it was like when they first arrived. Almost all our information came from a single, thin scrapbook buried in the bottom shelf of a cabinet in the far corner of our basement. Marie and I would sneak down and spend hours looking through the book. We read and reread newspaper clippings: an interview of my dad as a new immigrant and seminary student in Texas, an article about my mom living with her sponsor family in California when she first came over as a college student. We stared at the old black-and-white photographs of them as teenagers and young adults, surrounded by somber people we didn't know standing in front of strange-looking houses and wearing odd clothing. The scrapbook provided a window into a world we could barely understand. But since we knew it was a vital part of who our family was, we wanted whatever information we could find.

My parents didn't like to talk about their previous lives in Korea. Perhaps they were focused on having us be Americans, and remembering it may have been too painful. My mother was only fifteen years old when she fled across the North Korean border under the cover of night. Accompanying her aunt and carrying her five-year-old nephew on her back, she hoped the guide they hired would indeed take them across the border and not turn them in to the North Korean authorities. The rest of her family never made it out, except for a brother who made the trek to South Korea before her.

Never being able to see her own mother again haunted my mother. She would grow quiet and distant whenever someone brought up the topic. In the 1980s, we were able to travel to Korea and visit the demilitarized zone. My mom spent her time there silently staring into North Korea. She later told me she had been thinking about her mother. Today, as she battles Alzheimer's, almost every phone call with her has some variation on this conversation: "Did you know that your grandmother just died? No one told me!"

My father's family had made it out from North Korea much earlier, and for the most part they were able to rebuild their lives in Seoul. Because of his dream to come to America, my dad worked hard to learn English. His efforts paid off. During the Korean War, he worked as a translator for American officers, a plum assignment that eventually led to an opportunity to immigrate to the States.

My dad liked to tell stories of meeting the GIs who fueled his desire to come to America. They became an important source for his vision of the country, and his encounters with them reinforced his belief that the United States was a magical land of opportunity and wonder. He used to fish the soldiers' old *Life* magazines out of the trash because he liked to look at the pictures. One day he opened the magazine and saw a lovely rose color in one of the ads. It was the most beautiful color he had ever seen. "America must be a very special place," he thought, "if people can throw away a magazine with such a beautiful color in it." He clipped out the piece of the page with the color on it and kept it with him for the rest of the war as a constant reminder of his goal to someday make it to the United States.

My dad would describe how the GIs would share their meat with him sometimes, which was particularly meaningful because meat was such a scarce commodity, especially during the war. He would take the precious piece they had generously offered and slice it very thinly to make it last longer. With a wistful smile he would rec-reate the slow, purposeful slicing movements for us so we could relive the sacred moment. He loved the American meat and told us he knew it was special because it had its own name: Spam.

My dad envied the US soldiers simply because they were Americans and were able to live in America. His childhood and young adult years had been spent in a country ravaged by Japanese occupation and then war. During the Korean War, Seoul was captured, liberated, and recaptured multiple times by the North Koreans. He told us that during one period of North Korean occu-pation, he spent months hidden in the basement of his sister's house in Seoul to avoid being captured and forced to serve in the North Korean army. In that basement, he spent his time reading by candlelight. He subsisted on millet-and-water gruel. Even rice was too expensive. We would later discover this experience was behind one of the recurring lessons for his children. With a flourish, he would demonstrate to my sister and me how he could use his chopsticks to pick the last grain of rice from his bowl in order not to waste anything, admonishing us for leaving so much food on our plates.

One event seemed to encapsulate his thoughts and emotions during this period of his life. In the middle of one of the North Korean advances and American retreats from Seoul, he briefly came out of his sister's house to see the US soldiers getting into their trucks and abandoning the city. As he watched them withdraw, he wished he was like them and could just leave on one of their trucks. But he knew it was impossible. He was not an American like they were, so he did the only thing he could do. He went back into the basement.

For my dad, the United States meant a new life, one filled with potential and devoid of war and foreign oppression. It was a place where he could choose what he wanted to do and where his children would escape the suffering he had experienced. America was strong, the best country in the world, and he wanted to belong to it.

My dad realized his dream, largely thanks to the efforts of an American officer he met while translating for an army Bible study. He and my mother were able to come to the United States shortly after the fighting stopped. They got married, had my oldest brother, Victor, and immediately set about becoming Americans. They would always love the country of their birth. But they also knew that in coming to a new country, they were cutting off precious ties with the land where they grew up. They were making a commitment to their new country. They were not only living in America; they had to think of themselves *as* Americans.

M y parents knew it would not be easy, but they were willing to do whatever was needed to make a new life in the United States. As much as they loved Korea, they had chosen to be someplace else. They understood they would not simply be two individuals coming to a new country. They wanted to belong.

Because of their intense desire to be a part of America and the American way of life, they eagerly pursued assimilation. This was particularly true with regard to raising their children. Unlike many first-generation Korean immigrants, they did not teach us the Korean language. Although my father still wanted traditional Korean food, my siblings and I mostly ate American food at home like our classmates (and yes, my mother often had to cook two dinners each day). The only physical pieces of evidence of their native culture on display in our home were a few Korean artifacts: a single scroll hanging on the living room wall, a doll on a side table, and a small gong in the basement. Until I left for college, we rarely talked about Korea. My siblings and I lived and breathed America. We spoke only English, read American books, and watched American TV, dreaming of the next steps to take in our lives in this country.

My parents wanted our family to belong to America. In this longing to be a part of something bigger than themselves, they were hardly alone. We all have a fundamental need to be a part of something, to identify with a group, to be accepted into something larger. We are driven to identify with something beyond ourselves. We are created that way. Being a part of a group gives us a sense of security and purpose. And so we identify ourselves by these groups, whether they represent our nationality, our race, our gender, our age, our political affiliations, our favorite sports team, or our common hobbies and interests.

The Christian identity is a corporate identity. Paul uses the image of the body to tell the individual parts who they are in Christ. The flip side of this image is that an essential aspect of their individual identity flows *from* their corporate identity. They are *together* members of Christ's body. This means they have relationships with and responsibilities to a group and to Christ. Underlying all this is an important fact we must not miss: Paul says that Christ's followers are not only like a body but *are* a body.

> For just as the body is one and has many members, and all the members of the body, though many, are one body, so it is with Christ. (1 Cor. 12:12 ESV)

> You are the body of Christ. (1 Cor. 12:27)

This point is worth pausing for. Paul wants us to grasp something absolutely critical. Before we talk about what we do, he wants us to know who we are. He wants us to understand the nature of our new identity. We *are* a body. We are Christ's body. Christ *is* one and many, and each of us is a part of that one and many.

This is more than a nice image to encourage us to cooperate and get along. It's more than a teaching tool. Paul is talking about something real and true, something that has already happened. This is *who we are*, and *who we are* has real substance. The reason we are one body is because God's Spirit has made us into something new. As Paul explains, "For in one Spirit we were all baptized into one body—Jews or Greeks, slaves or free—and all were made to drink of one Spirit" (1 Cor. 12:13 ESV).

This is why 1 Corinthians 12 is not simply a collection of marching orders. As mentioned earlier, the only command comes at the end of the chapter in verse 31. The main point is not to tell us how the parts of the body should act, that is, by contributing to the whole. Paul will give specific instructions about this later.[2] But first, he is more concerned with instructing the Corinthians about their new group identity: what the body of Christ is, how everyone is a member, and how this oneness is part of our new life in the Spirit. This reality shapes how we think about ourselves. Every part needs to know that it belongs. Every part needs to know that the other parts belong. This group identity is also important because what—or *who*—we belong to makes all the difference.

CHAPTER 5

THE POWER OF CORPORATE IDENTITY

For my parents, a critical step in belonging to America was gaining citizenship. Being a citizen meant they had assurance they could stay, so they did what they could to make this happen.

As the only anesthesiologist in our region, my dad worked tremendously hard, especially since he was trying to demonstrate that he should be allowed to remain in the country. He wanted America to see that he was fulfilling a critical need. In addition to his regular work hours, he frequently went in for emergency procedures. I have countless memories of watching him take out the snowblower in the middle of a frigid night to clear the driveway so he could go to the hospital. After he returned, he would try to catch a couple hours of sleep so he would be ready for his regular day of surgeries.

Dad was called away most frequently during holidays.

It was uncanny how often it would happen just after he placed a knife on the Thanksgiving turkey or Christmas roast, ready to make the first slice. Sometimes he would respond with humor. With a little smile in his eyes, he would playfully demonstrate how many of those emergencies occurred when inebriated people who aren't used to carving massive pieces of meat with large knives end up slicing more than the bird. At other times, he'd quietly lament how people would often suffer the effects of too much celebratory food and drink. Whatever the reasons, the result was the same for our family: holiday dinner without Dad. We learned to assume his seat at the table would be empty. He never complained, though his shoulders drooped a little more each year when he got that inevitable phone call.

As hard as my dad worked, both of my parents knew their ability to stay in the country was tenuous. Before they became citizens, the threat of being deported hung over them constantly. One enduring family story was about receiving a deportation notice the same day they brought my newborn sister home from the hospital. My mother cried, wondering how they could go back to Korea with a new baby. My father wondered what would happen to their American-born children who were not Korean citizens.

But this incident would become just another part of their lives as immigrants wanting to find a new life in the United States. All of these stories were woven into the larger story of our family identity. In those days, my father's custom was to take a photo of everyone standing in front of the house whenever there was a significant family occasion, and bringing my sister home for the first time was no exception. When we look at that photo now, we don't say, "Look how cute Marie was!" We say, "Yeah, that's the day Mom and Dad found out they were going to be deported." So much of our lives was understood in the context of my parents' efforts to be members of their new country.

In the end, they were very fortunate. Our US Representative introduced a bill that enabled them to stay. They were given a reprieve, and eventually, after being in the country more than a dozen years and having four children, they became citizens.

This was a momentous occasion, and it happened right around the time I was born. My dad would later tell me that by the time I joined the family, in contrast to my sister's inauspicious introduction to the world, he was finally able to relax. Things were going to be okay. They had achieved what they had long dreamed of. Never again would they have to worry about being forced to leave. In their eyes, they had made it. They finally belonged.

※

My parents took their citizenship very seriously. They considered themselves first of all Americans (and Minnesotans), and while they were still very interested in what happened in Korea, they were definitely on Team USA.

My parents' identification as Americans was palpable, and it intensified after they became citizens. It drove how they thought of themselves and how they acted. They were grateful for the resources and opportunities that were now available to them and their children and eager to contribute to their country.

When people talk about unity, they often focus on a common goal, for example, combatting racism, electing a certain presidential candidate, or signing petitions. But I rarely find much of a discussion about unity as an expression of our identity.[1] I don't hear how we have a common "name" or understanding that captures who we are and what we are about, that reflects how we are to see ourselves as members of a new group.

Perhaps it's because unity is too easily identified with an action—to unify. But for Paul, unity, or oneness, is who we *are*. And who we are informs what we do.

We see the power of corporate identity everywhere. No one needs to tell a student to cheer for their own basketball team or persuade them to buy an expensive sweatshirt proudly bearing their school's name.

National pride is another example. The nation was transfixed by the 1980 US Olympic hockey team's gold medal run, even being called "the most celebrated moment in American Winter Olympics history."[2] For a brief period, Americans shared a dynamic common identity that brought us together. We saw ourselves and each other as a united nation of Americans.

A more sobering example was 9/11. That day became indelibly etched in our collective memory, one of those "Where were you when it happened?" moments. Seeing the attack made us *all* Americans. Even if the effect was fleeting, on that horrific day and for a brief period after, people saw each other as neighbors and were motivated to help one another.

A profound sense of togetherness based on shared identity is a big part of what Paul is after. The corporate identity of the Christian community was not simply a nice teaching point—it was a critical reality. The followers of Jesus were "one" (Gal. 3:28). Since the term *unity* means different things to different people, it may be helpful to also focus on what it means that we are "one."

This is our identity as Christians. Paul doesn't say we need to *become* one. He says we *are* one. This has already happened in the Spirit. It's an established fact. And now, the believers need to know why this oneness matters. Everyone belongs, no matter what part of the body they are. We are so intimately connected with each other that we can be exquisitely attuned to the other members and share in their experience:

> But God has so composed the body, giving greater honor to the part that lacked it, that there may be no division in the body, but that the members may have the same care for one another. If one member suffers, all suffer together; if one member is honored, all rejoice together. (1 Cor. 12:24–26 ESV)

Again, Paul is not giving us a command to be unified. He is not telling us to rejoice or mourn with one another to effect a form of togetherness. He is saying that God has *made* us a unified body so that we *can* empathize with one another in these ways. His point here is not about an action but about a state of being. Who we are will lead to what we are to do. Who we are matters because we are *already* connected.

Think about this in light of your own physical body. What happens when one part of your body is suffering, such as an excruciating migraine headache, a broken bone, or an intense stomachache? Everything else comes to a halt as you give your attention to that injured member. You don't have to tell yourself to pay attention to it. You do it because your pain sensors make sure you don't ignore it.

The image of the body signifies an intimate, organic interconnection among its parts. How we respond to pain in the body is perhaps the most obvious illustration of this kind of unity. The flip side can serve as a warning to us: when the body doesn't feel or respond to pain, it means that something is very wrong. In fact, there is a medical condition known as congenital analgesia, when someone cannot feel pain in their body. People suffering from this may be able to feel touch or pressure, but not pain. They don't know when something harmful is happening. They may not realize they are putting their hand on a hot stove or that they have a broken bone that needs to be set. Young children may bite and chew on themselves without realizing they are harming themselves. Toothaches and other painful bodily sensations that signal we need to get treatment can go unnoticed until it is too late. Without an awareness of what is happening to their bodies, people who have congenital analgesia don't realize they need to care for the afflicted parts or stop doing something damaging.

God formed the body of Christ as one interconnected, organic whole, yet this doesn't guarantee we will experience intimacy. We may have our own form of congenital analgesia. We tend to begin with the *functional* value of the body of Christ, telling every person they should contribute to the body, but this is step two for Paul. He emphasizes understanding who we *are* as the foundation for what we do. Paul wants us to see that we are first of all people genuinely connected with one another, who can then care for one another because we are members of the same whole.

We can see this connection in statements such as when Paul says the members of the body should rejoice together as well as suffer together (1 Cor. 12:26). It's easy to see how caring applies to pain and suffering together as one body, but Paul tells us it is equally important to rejoice together. And why not? When something good happens to us, it's better when we share it with others. Celebrating a birthday, a promotion, or a child's personal milestone makes the occasion that much more special. We were made to be connected, in good times and bad.

Paul wanted the church to grow in their understanding of their new corporate identity. Why? So they would be able to live in that existence as the Spirit worked in their hearts to overcome old hostilities and prejudices and instead live in Christ's humility and God's grace with one another. After all, just because we are one, it doesn't mean we'll *act* like we are one. We are not seeking to create a unity that does not exist, as much as to discover, develop, and deepen what is already there.

In Paul's day, being a member of the body meant you belonged, but it also meant that the other members "belonged" to you as an aspect of being connected.[3] "Belonging" in this sense also communicates responsibility, recognizing and appreciating what is already a part of you.[4] We naturally take care of what belongs to us, not just because it is useful for us, but because we have a natural affection for what we see as connected to us.[5] The more we perceive our organic connection to something or someone, that they matter to us, the more we want to care for that person or thing. When the authorities informed my husband and me that wildfires were heading our direction and we needed to evacuate our home, we instinctively grabbed our personal photos, important papers, and the dogs. Those things mattered to us. They were valued. No one needed to tell us to save them—we just did it. When we see an ambulance in front of a neighbor's house, we check in on them. We care for them and want to know how they are doing.

Even mundane incidents illustrate our draw toward others when we realize we have a connection with them. Many years ago, my sister was studying in Paris, and my parents and I joined her for a vacation. We went out to dinner at one of her favorite places, a little restaurant called Le Soufflé, where almost everything on the menu was (surprise!) a soufflé. At one point during our dinner, we realized that the people at the table next to ours happened to live near us. And by "near" I don't just mean the

United States, or even our state, but they lived in our city (which was Minneapolis at the time, since my parents had moved out of our hometown). In a little restaurant on the other side of the world were some people we were connected to.

This newfound awareness of our relatedness—a simple geographic connection—made us all the more interesting to each other. We were thrilled by the coincidence of being halfway around the world and meeting people who were practically our neighbors. We spent the rest of the evening talking about our city and sharing our travel experiences. When dinner was finally finished, we left the restaurant recounting the unexpectedly delightful encounter, marveling at the chances of meeting each other in a small restaurant in Paris.

Knowing we were connected made all the difference. Our relationship flowed from the discovery of our commonality. In a similar way, rather than commanding the Corinthians to "be united," Paul is telling them, "You have something really important in common. You already are connected, even if you've never met. You are one in Christ!" Simply instructing them to be nicer to one another isn't going to cut it. Their affections for one another must be kindled. That is why Paul spends so much time describing their group identity and what it means for them to be one. They may not be living in unity at the moment because they are consumed by self-interest, but the reality is that God has made them to be a body. Paul wants them to become who they already are. Being one is who we are—and who we are to become.

※

I knew we were part of the community in Minnesota. Yet it was made known to us that we were not fully part of it. We didn't fully belong. And we were further isolated because our extended family were mostly back in Korea, limiting our family unit to just my parents, my three siblings, and me. My father would write and send money back to his relatives in Korea, but in our daily lives, our family began and ended with us. Growing up, my dad's sister visited once, but I was too young to remember it now. I only know it happened because I saw a photo of us with her at our house. A large portrait of my dad's father hung over the couch in his study. But my dad rarely talked about his father. We didn't really think of him as our grandfather. Rather, he was our dad's dad, a stern and mysterious person in the painting whose eyes would follow Marie and me around the room, making sure we behaved.

To compensate for our isolation, my parents tried to give us some semblance of an extended family. People who were particularly significant in our lives were given honorary aunt and uncle titles, like Uncle Howard and Aunt Marie, who were my parents' neighbors when they first came to town. Even after my parents moved to a different side of town, we would continue to spend time with them. Uncle Howard would take Marie and me to get ice cream cones at the Bridgeman's near their house, which was a special treat because my health-conscious mother only allowed us to have the then-current health fad, low-fat ice milk. Uncle Howard taught me an important lesson in personal responsibility the time I licked mine too hard and the lone, single scoop fell off, landing with a distinct plop on the parking lot asphalt. He refused my request to buy me another to replace my now ice-cream-less cone, telling me I should be more careful next time. Aunt Marie, whom my sister was named after, liked to knit and made my siblings and me beautiful sweaters when we graduated from high school.

Yet despite the constant presence of people like Uncle Howard and Aunt Marie in our lives, I didn't grasp what those titles really meant. *Aunt* and *uncle* signified people close to our family, but who also weren't family. I didn't really understand what it meant to have relatives beyond your immediate family. My high school BFF would talk about her cousin. Years later I would meet my own cousins, but at the time I just couldn't grasp the concept. How could someone be and not be a member of your family?

Our isolation from extended family meant that we developed a strong sense of our immediate family as our core family unit. We were a tight group, and people were allowed into our little circle only very carefully. The outside world was something other, something to be protected against.

This shaped our family's corporate identity. People outside our family were often viewed with suspicion. This was particularly true when we traveled. My father saw other people as "foreign bodies." To my mother they were "strangers," to be guarded against by our tight family circle. Our house was a refuge that kept us safe inside its walls. The fact that houses in northern Minnesota are built like fortresses to keep out the bitter cold only reinforced the sense that our home protected us from the hostile world.

One incident echoes in my mind and perhaps sheds some light on our family mindset. The connection may be exaggerated, likely the product of my sometimes overactive imagination. But I can't help thinking that it reflects how we experienced life in those days.

Marka was a German Shepherd. She was small by Shepherd standards, but effective. She was great with us, but she did *not* like other people, especially those who came to our house. One of the things Marka liked to do was snarl and claw at the window next to the front door whenever anyone rang the doorbell. Since the door was directly at the top of a flight of stairs, upon hearing the chime she would come charging up the stairs to get a running leap at the window, where she could display her full snarling glory. It was a little embarrassing, but we didn't know what do to about it, and we were reluctant to use our neighbor's method of dog training, which was beating his Siberian husky with a shovel.

Marka especially liked to show off for the poor postal worker bringing packages to our door. One day, I came home from school and found glass all over the floor. Apparently, the postal employee rang the doorbell, and per her usual habit, Marka bolted up the stairs. This time, instead of terrifying him from behind the window, she crashed right through the glass. Fortunately, she didn't make it all the way through. We had multiple-pane windows, which not only kept the Minnesota cold out but also kept lunging German Shepherds in. Luckily for him, one pane held.

Years later, I remember watching a show about how dogs reflect their owners' personalities (a phenomenon which might be related to that odd reality that pets can often look like their owners).[6] While I realize this may be a stretch since German Shepherds have a naturally protective personality, I can't help but wonder if Marka was picking up on our family vibe as well. In our home there was always tension when we thought or talked about the outside world—a constant need to be on guard and a longing for a protected space to rest, a place to feel safe. Perhaps Marka was responding to our wants—our desire to keep this part of our life secure and separate from the rest of the world, a world that often seemed hostile and where we often suffered rejection.

I grew up with a sense that the only truly safe place was with my family. You could spend time with others, but in the end, you needed to come back home where you could relax and know things would be okay. The outside world was a threat. And while you might need to venture out from time-to-time to do the necessary things of life, and you always held out the hope of being able to fit in somewhere, what you really wanted at the end of the day was to come home, shut the door, and be left alone.

Our failure to integrate with the rest of the world intensified our group identity, at least in my parents' minds. My siblings and I heard endless recitations of, "Family is all you have," and "No matter what, the four of you kids have to stick together." Everything was family. The outside world could be harsh and rejecting, so my parents insisted we stay together to make sure we'd all be okay.

Over time, I came to understand that not all families were like ours. When I would visit my friend with the cousin, I was surprised at how her house was the complete opposite of ours. Instead of tightly closed doors and a sharp distinction between inside and outside, her house seemed to be made of revolving doors and porous borders. When I visited her at her home, I would walk through the front door, a door that would swing shut but would not stay closed for long. There was constant activity, people going in and out, moving seamlessly from inside to outside and back again. The house was lively, filled with chattering kids. Friends dropped off school books on the kitchen table and headed to the refrigerator for a snack or went back outside to hang out and play kickball in the street.

My friend would tell me that her cousin and her siblings' friends were always dropping by, which astounded me. Unannounced? Without time to plan and make sure the house was ready for "company" (as my mother would call those who visited)? I tried to hide my astonishment. Her house radiated a sense of welcome, of relationships, of being a natural continuation of the larger world. Our house, by contrast, was like a spacious and nicely appointed bomb shelter, with a paradoxical air of tension and relief, where we could let down our guard even as we defended against outside hostility.

Yet despite the dysfunctional nature of this family dynamic, I understand—at least partly—why my parents reacted the way they did. As much as they wanted to be Americans, there was always the injury of not being fully accepted by their adopted country. The piece of paper proclaiming their citizenship did not always translate into acceptance.

My father continued to speak glowingly about America and the opportunities the country offered. He would always say it was the best country on earth. But every once in a while, when he would let down his guard, I caught a glimpse of deeper emotions and pain. I remember he once spoke quietly but bitterly about children at the hospital who pointed at him and shouted, "You look like an ape!" while their parents stood by and did nothing. I was shocked because it was so unlike him to say anything negative about life in the United States. But that was all he said, and then the moment disappeared, like a pebble that falls into a smooth lake and vanishes with barely a ripple.

⌇

As much as they loved and were loyal to their adopted country, I believe my parents' feelings of displacement compelled them to make our home and family their refuge, the one place they could escape the tension. Perhaps, if they had felt more accepted, our house would have more naturally reflected a sense of openness and welcome, evidence of a corporate identification with the community. Perhaps our home would have looked more

like my friend's house with the revolving doors. Instead, my parents retreated further into the identity they had, even as they continued to seek ways to integrate.

This was their lifelong dilemma. They tried fervently to assimilate, but couldn't, or at least not as much as they had hoped. So, paradoxically, they reached a point where they didn't belong anywhere. They were never completely accepted in their new country, nor did they fit in with the country of their birth. They had been in America long enough to have adapted to many of its customs, mannerisms, and even accents. But this distanced them from the culture of their homeland. When my siblings and I would visit Korea later in life as adults, my mother would complain to us that she no longer felt like she fit in there. She was embarrassed when people would say they couldn't understand her because she was no longer as fluent in her native language and spoke with an American accent. But in the United States, people would have trouble understanding her English and comment on her Korean accent. My parents' displacement was similar to that of other immigrants. But because we lived in northern Minnesota, far from other Korean families, they had no one else who shared their experience.

Although their response to their isolation produced its own problems, I sympathize with my parents' intense focus on protecting our immediate family. They couldn't go back to Korea, but they didn't feel fully a part of America, either. Because we all need a place to belong, they poured their energy into our family unit. Here was a place they could fit in.

CHAPTER 6

THE CHURCH AS A FAMILY

Families are a natural unit. Although we may have very different experiences with our own families, we generally know what families are supposed to be like. We expect them to be warm, loving, accepting, and protective. Families are meant to nurture us and provide us with security. Families are where we can grow into what we were meant to be.

It should not surprise us, then, that there is another significant New Testament image that speaks to the intimate nature of our relationships within the Christian community. We are the family of God.[1]

In antiquity, the family was considered the "tightest unit of loyalty and affection."[2] The significance of family is easy to miss in our Western individualistic society, which prizes autonomy and self-expression. To understand the context of the New Testament, we need to first learn to appreciate the strong group- and family-oriented assumptions of the world of the early church. If we don't, we can miss a lot of the power behind the new community created by the gospel.

Our culture spends a lot of time telling us to go for what we deserve, to know our rights, and to be true to ourselves. Often this revolves around an underlying assumption: our ultimate goal is to have a fulfilling life as an individual.

But in Jesus's day, people thought of themselves first and foremost as members of a group—and they were accountable to that group for their actions and their life overall. The group, and in particular, the family unit, had priority over its individual members, and people's decisions were oriented to the group's goals.[3]

This is why Jesus's teaching about the disciples' need to forsake fathers and mothers and brothers and sisters was, to put it mildly, scandalous.[4] Jesus was asking his disciples to compromise their family relationships, to change their primary loyalties.[5] He declared he was going to turn households against one another, setting sons against fathers and daughters against mothers (Matt. 10:35; Luke 12:53). He said his true family was "those who hear God's word and put it into practice" (Luke 8:21; see also Mark 3:31–35). Jesus told a man *not* to bury the man's father before following him (Matt. 8:21–22; Luke 9:59–60), putting allegiance to Jesus above the commandment to honor father and mother (Ex. 20:12; Deut. 6:5).[6]

But it is not simply that it was outrageous for Jesus to

say these things about their families. Jesus was also saying the disciples were members of a *new* family. But what kind of community was he forming? In creating a new family, Jesus was not abandoning the family but rather saying his followers were in a greater family.

As with the body of Christ, the family of God is not simply a heart-warming thought or an abstract theological truth. It is a reality that creates deep community, fulfilling our natural human longings to belong somewhere. The community of believers was not meant to be *like* a family; they *were* a family.[7] The truth of their new bond—created by God—formed the foundation for relationships marked by unwavering loyalty, care, and intimacy.

Though they may not have been connected in the natural sense of physical blood ties, they were now connected by something even more profound and powerful: they were members of the family of God through the blood of Christ—brothers and sisters marked as fellow sharers of God's Spirit (1 Cor. 12:13), partakers of the same grace from Jesus (Phil. 1:7), and partners in the gospel (1:5).

One striking aspect of Paul's letters is his genuine affection for the believers. He writes to the Thessalonians of his "intense longing" to see them (1 Thess. 2:17) because they "had become very dear" to him (1 Thess. 2:8 ESV) and were his "glory and joy" (1 Thess. 2:20). He tells the Philippians they are his brothers and sisters, "whom I love and long for" (Phil. 4:1). Even though he does not seem to have visited the Roman congregation, nevertheless, he tells them, "I long to see you" (Rom. 1:11).

Elsewhere he speaks of his abounding love for Christ's people (1 Thess. 3:12).[8]

These were not superficial or gratuitous words. Paul tells the Philippians that he longs for them "with the affection of Christ Jesus" (Phil. 1:8). The phrase that Paul uses here refers to those parts of the body, such as the heart, that were the source of deep emotions such as anger and love. And in connecting this with Christ, Paul is in effect saying his affection for them is grounded in a love that comes from Christ himself.[9]

Today, we tend to prize romantic love as the ultimate expression of a close and intimate relationship. But in the time of the New Testament, the closest bond was between siblings.[10] This helps us better understand the impact of Paul's ubiquitous use of brother and sister terminology in his letters.[11] As brothers and sisters in this new family, the believers were connected with the deepest obligations and affections, as those who shared the same Father.[12]

In 1 Corinthians 8, we see an example of how this worked itself out in daily life. Paul speaks of the need to make a personal sacrifice to avoid causing another believer to "stumble" and injure their relationship with God. This specific situation revolves around eating meat in pagan temples. Although Paul says that eating the meat itself is intrinsically harmless, it may cause problems for another believer who may think it still has real connections with idol worship (1 Cor. 8:4, 7–8). The "weak" believer is acting from a mistaken belief, but Paul still calls for the other person to abstain (1 Cor. 8:9–13).

This is about more than giving up a meal. To withdraw from an occasion like this could lead to ostracism from society.[13] But Paul says that one's connection to a brother or sister must come first. His sense of personal commitment and responsibility is apparent as the person is described not simply as *a* brother but as *my* brother (1 Cor. 8:13).[14] Paul does not give a command here. He appeals to family loyalty. One should make this sacrifice to help one's brother.

What is astounding, however, is not only the sacrifice but also the person one might need to sacrifice for. The church now included Jew *and* gentile, rich *and* poor, male *and* female, slave *and* free. It's one thing to suffer for a close friend or for a preferred family member, but suffering for someone you have always believed is inferior to you? Someone who might have been your enemy? The barriers to relationship within the new Christian community reflected the challenges of bringing together very different people who resided on opposite ends of a stratified social spectrum. And yet these people were now "one" and called to be like Christ to each other.

⇁⍀⎮⍳

The big question Paul faced, and the question we all face, was how to live out the truth of that oneness. The interesting thing about families is that they often include people who might not naturally get along, and yet that can never change the very real ties that exist.

As I mentioned earlier, one of my father's favorite hobbies was taking pictures of the family standing in front of our house on special occasions. Our family albums are full of pictures of us dutifully posing. You can almost always find us in the same formation—my older brothers in back, my sister and me in front—just with different backgrounds, wearing different clothing, and at different stages of life.

But one photo has a slightly different setup. In this photo my sister, who is about four or five, is closer to the camera, hunched over and clutching her stomach. In the back is my brother Len, who is about ten, in his proper position with a huge grin on his face for having just punched his younger sister in the stomach.

Len and Marie did not always get along growing up, but that did not change the fact that they were family. And in the New Testament, being one—as a family, as the body of Christ—describes both a state of being and a potential. This is who we are, whether or not we act like it. This is also who we want to become.

The road to deep unity for the new Christian community was just that—a road. It was unrealistic to expect that everyone would instantly get along and have perfect patience and understanding with each other. We are all different. We are all human. We are all sinners.

It should not be surprising that there would be clashes, misunderstandings, and relational tension. Jesus is taking people who do not get along, do not think they should associate with each other, and might even be enemies, and now telling them that they are one big family.

When we look around at our current strife and divisions, we can easily say, "Well, you say Paul believes we

are one, but it doesn't seem like we are really unified."
And that is correct. Paul says our fundamental unity is
accomplished by God in the Spirit (1 Cor. 12:13). It is a
reality that exists no matter what we do. But acting in a
unified manner is a very different matter. Paul's goal is for
believers to grow *into* the oneness that we already have,
to become who we are, to become attuned to the Spirit
so we can manifest in our daily lives what we already are
in the Spirit. No program, policy, or rule can accomplish
this. Perhaps these can be useful as guides, but only to a
certain extent. Only the Spirit of God can overcome our

natural hardness of heart, enabling us to truly love those who belong to us and to understand that God's ways are far above our own ways (Isa. 55:8–9).[15]

Identity is the starting point. But since we do not always realize the implications of being one body and the family of God, Paul enjoins us to think deeply about who we are. He knows that the power of that identity can lead to true loving relationships among brothers and sisters in Christ, that it can take those who used to be at odds with one another—Jew and gentile, slave and free, male and female—and make them into a community that is fully reconciled with God and one another. This is our corporate sanctification.

A popular saying among my college students is that love is an action, not a feeling. True enough, especially if you're thinking about those feelings as butterflies in the stomach when you look at the object of your affection. Love is being able to do the right thing, being able to sacrifice even when the one you love lets you down and perhaps betrays you. Love is what God did for us when Jesus died on the cross (John 3:16).

But if love is more than a feeling, we should clarify that it is also more than an action. Because for Paul love is *connected with an attachment*, an attachment that leads to caring, even great affection. Paul's great hymn on love comes in 1 Corinthians 13, famously used in weddings everywhere. But it isn't first and foremost about marital love. It follows from 1 Corinthians 12, Paul's description of the body of Christ and the intimate relationships among the members who are able to feel each other's joys and sorrows.[16] This connectedness—as members of the same body and brothers and sisters in Christ—was the foundation of his great affection for his Jewish and gentile brothers and sisters and fueled his willingness to make joyful sacrifices on their behalf.

If all this is true, then understanding the nature of our corporate belonging is absolutely essential. Later in life, my mother started an agency in Minnesota dedicated to helping Korean seniors who were having difficulty adjusting to life in the United States. One of the things her agency did was help elderly Korean immigrants understand and pass the US citizenship test. At the ceremony where they were sworn in as citizens, they would wave small American flags and cry because it meant so much to them. It was a testimony to what they had sacrificed to come here and what the country represented to them, their children, and their hopes and dreams.

Our belonging in Christ is more profound than American citizenship. It is our reality in Jesus, where we are bound together by the Spirit. This truth—that we are members of Christ himself, fellow sharers in the Spirit, the family of God—enables us to love one another, even though our differences are very real and very deep. Realizing this truth is how we find the grace and courage to overcome difficulties that seem insurmountable. And it is how we can live out what God made us to be.

CHAPTER 7

SEEING AND BEING SEEN

I didn't play with Barbie dolls when I was growing up. It wasn't because the only ones available at the time were White. What bothered me was more anatomical than skin-related. Barbie just looked weird to me. She seemed abnormally long and skinny (but somehow still very curvaceous), and she had stiff, immovable limbs that couldn't do anything but strike a perfect model pose. I was confused by her practically nonexistent waist and didn't understand why she had to stand on her tip toes all the time. I didn't share her obsession with clothes, hair, and makeup—much less that guy Ken who was way too old-looking for my taste. Instead of Barbie, my sister and I played with Josie and Janice West dolls. As flat-chested prepubescent cowgirls, not only did they look more like real people, but their moveable limbs also enabled them to do fun things like beat up the prepubescent boy dolls.

Maybe I never thought about Barbie's skin color because there were so many other things that distracted me. I recall how it was a big deal back in the early '80s when Mattel started making Barbies of different ethnicities. I suppose if I had been more into the world of Barbie, I would have appreciated a doll that looked a bit more like me. On the other hand, my reaction shows how much I believed there was only one way to be. My life was so saturated with Whiteness as normal and non-Whiteness as abnormal that it didn't even occur to me that there could be a Barbie that looked like me.

⎯╱╲╲⎯

I've heard people say that because we are all one in Christ now, race shouldn't matter. But I disagree. Race does matter. It is very much a part of who I am because it is how God made me. We may all share the same Spirit, but in the body of Christ we are very different. Scripture is full of references that talk about how God knows us individually. I was known by God even before I was born (Jer. 1:5), as he is the one who secretly knit me together in my mother's womb (Ps. 139:15–16) and has even the hairs of my head numbered (Matt. 10:30; Luke 12:7). I am "fearfully and wonderfully made" (Ps. 139:14), and my particular days were ordained before I took my first breath (Ps. 139:16).

We don't need to choose between our individual identity and being part of a greater community. Nor is one aspect necessarily more important than the other. Instead, I can ponder the mysterious way God made me both a unique self and a self in community. And I'm not alone in thinking this way. Carl Trueman says this is the "quintessential problem of identity in the modern era," that is, "how can I simultaneously be myself and belong to a larger social group?"[1]

So instead of asking, *Does race matter?* the better question may be, *How does race matter?* Does God have a purpose in race and ethnicity, and could that purpose be a key to what kingdom unity is all about? I doubt these questions have easy answers—there rarely are easy answers for these kinds of things. However, I suspect the solution lies somewhere in understanding what it means for a person to be created and loved by God. I am important to God individually in all the ways he has made me. At the same time I am a part of various communities. I am a member of the human race and also the family of God.

I find that trying to figure out how race impacts who I am is not a linear process where insight builds on insight until one day I attain complete enlightenment and suddenly everything falls into place and fits. Rather, it is a journey that cannot be easily defined or distilled into simplistic formulas. It contains disparate threads, neverending layers, and seeming contradictions. But at its core, this understanding gets deeper and richer the more I see what it means to be a unique individual born into a complicated and sin-filled world that I share with other unique and sinful individuals. Minimally, it means I need to know what it means to be human and how to live with other humans.

In school I was constantly ramping up my efforts to show my classmates I was just like them. I participated in school activities, kept up with all the latest TV shows (back when there were only three channels and everyone watched the same shows), and expressed all the proper opinions of our teachers. In other words, I tried to do all the things that my classmates did to fit in—at least the ones that were legal. Although it wasn't the most noble way to deal with my situation, it gave me a means to accept what I couldn't change. In the end, as much as I wished it were different, I could not escape the fact that I was Asian in a very non-Asian world.

So my race was continually an issue, as much as I desperately wished that weren't the case. But race was only the surface-level problem, an external matter that covered over the personal pain. Ultimately, the sensitive core struck by repeated rejection had to do with something else—my sense of personhood, what it means to be created in God's image, and my profound need to have that personhood seen.

The need to be seen by others applies to more than our racial identity or ethnicity, for what matters most to us goes far deeper than our skin color or cultural background. We can deny or overlook someone's personhood in many ways. We may do so despite the best of intentions, but the effect is still the same. We objectify the person, and do not see them for who they are.

A few years ago I met with a former student who

made me aware of something I hadn't considered. David is a delightful person, blessed with a cheerful and exuberant personality and love of people. He is bright and determined. Moreover, he has a remarkable singing voice, and one of his greatest loves is performing before a packed audience who recognize and appreciate God's gift of music.

David is also severely visually impaired, and he has been so since birth. He can occasionally see light and shadows if the conditions are just right, but that is all. He uses a screen reader that enables him to read material on a computer through a speech synthesizer. He uses a cane to get around or relies on the arm of a helpful friend. He is mindful of the challenges he faces, as well as the unfairness of his condition, but he finds great joy in singing, being with friends, and eating dessert.

One of the challenges he faces is getting others to see beyond his visual impairment. When he meets people, they often want to pray for his healing. Their intentions are good, but David has found many of these experiences somewhat disconcerting. The problem, as he explained it to me, is that when the first thing a person notices about him is his disability, they can become laser focused on that one thing.

This tends to be particularly true for the more enthusiastic healing-prayer folks, as all too often they immediately want to start praying for God to give him his sight. They may be sincere, but he ends up feeling that they don't see him as David, a person who has his own hopes, dreams, and fears, a person just like them.

Rather, they see him as a "blind person"—someone defined first and foremost by his disability. Sometimes people are so excited to pray for him that they just start praying, which can be rather unsettling if you can't see and people just come up to you and start poking their fingers in your eyes.

Yes, David would like to receive his sight. But he doesn't like the idea that he cannot be "whole" because of his condition, and that is the message he often receives from the way people treat him. He wants to be a person, not just a disability. When I asked him what he would like people to do, he told me he would like it if people would want to get to know him first and then, perhaps, ask if they can pray for him.

I'm not saying that having a disability or being Asian isn't a part of a person. I'm saying there is so much more to someone than their capacity to see or their skin color or some other physical feature. David must live with his impairment, but he has a greater need to be seen as a whole person. I too needed to be seen for more than my rejected Asianness. I wanted to know I was accepted for who I was, a human being in the image of God, and to know that there was worth just in being human. But the humanness I shared with others was often obscured by our racial differences. At times I received the message that I wasn't allowed that acceptance, that I was less human somehow because of my race.

We all want to be seen and known. A good part of our lives is impacted by that innate desire to be seen and then our response when we are rejected. This desire brings wholeness when it is fulfilled and pain and anger when it is denied or abused.

———※———

I was longing for something the psalmist tells us only God is able to give. Listen as the following psalm expresses how intimately God knows us:

> You have searched me, LORD,
>   and you know me.
> You know when I sit and when I rise;
>   you perceive my thoughts from afar.
> You discern my going out and my
>   lying down;
>   you are familiar with all my ways.
> Before a word is on my tongue
>   you, LORD, know it completely. (Ps.
>   139:1–4)

The psalmist tells us that God knows us from the very beginning, and he goes on to say that God has created our "inmost being" and was there when we were made "in the secret place" (Ps. 139:13–15). In short, he knows us inside and out. There is nothing we can hide from him; there is nothing about us that is not known to him.

In the New Testament we see how God's knowledge of us draws us to him. When Jesus calls Nathanael under the fig tree to be his disciple, Jesus says, "Here truly is an Israelite in whom there is no deceit." Nathanael asks in astonishment, "How do you know me?" (John 1:47–48). Jesus knows not only where Nathanael is sitting but also his true character. Nathanael's response is to declare Jesus the Son of God and the King of Israel—and to follow him.

There is great comfort in realizing that God knows us fully (1 Cor. 8:3; 13:12). He accepts us because he is the one who made us the way we are. But the flip side of this marvelous truth is that humans cannot know each other fully. We are the created, not the Creator. We do not have God's knowledge, and we certainly do not have God's patience and mercy.

This is where misunderstandings arise, among other things. We stereotype. We project. We misjudge people. We assume ill motives. We fail to see each other's humanity. We become ever more separated from one another, in big ways and small.

I spent five years in northern Indiana attending graduate school. One day my mother and I were out shopping in Amish territory. A popular attraction for tourists who visit the area is purchasing Amish quilts, and we wandered into a store where the person was selling some high-end quilts. If that sounds like an oxymoron for something associated with down-home simplicity, it did to us as well. These beautiful and intricately patterned quilts were not the kind you put on your guest room bed. They were typically intended for wall display, and the prices ran into the thousands of dollars.

The owner seemed particularly interested in us. As soon as he saw us enter the store, he abandoned the people he had been talking with and made a beeline straight for us. With great detail and enthusiasm, he described how special the quilts were. I was imagining an Amish sweatshop with rows of women in plain dresses and bonnets toiling away so he could make his big bucks. I noticed that even as new people came into the shop, he ignored them, continuing his energetic presentation to my mother and me. We finally got him to leave us alone by telling him we'd like to look around the store on our own, and my mother asked me why he had paid so much attention to us. Guessing, I told her he probably thought we were rich Japanese tourists willing to pay an exorbitant sum for a designer Amish quilt. I was correct. As we were leaving, he once again abruptly broke off from talking to another customer to give us an exuberant overhead wave from across the store, loudly shouting, "Sayonara!"

We dislike stereotyping, when someone assigns characteristics to another person just because they are members of a certain group. We know it can be harmful and hurtful. But I am also hesitant to reflexively condemn people for it because the reality is that I do my own stereotyping. In fact, we all do it.

A couple years ago, my stepdaughter and son-in-law moved to Nashville. As soon as they settled into their new city, they began dropping subtle hints.

"Wouldn't you like to be close to your grandchildren? You could come over all the time!"

"The house next door might be for sale. You should buy it!"

Being fairly astute people (this is what higher education

does for you), my husband and I realized they wanted us to move to Nashville. While it was a very attractive idea for us to be closer to them, one of my first thoughts was also, "But you live in the *South*." Thinking about moving to Tennessee gave me visions of people staring at me and calling me a "chink" everywhere I went. I felt a nervousness and dread that I hadn't experienced since childhood. But we took the plunge and made the move (more on that later), and so far, things have been . . . well, just fine. I had to adjust my own preconceived ideas about people in the South. Some expectations have proved fairly accurate, such as our neighbor who invited my husband over for some homemade banana moonshine (the banana part not withstanding). But I haven't encountered stares or comments and have rather enjoyed how friendly people have been.

Sadly, it was easy for me to stereotype an entire region as backward, ignorant, and racist. But living here and meeting real people has proven me wrong, at least in the area where we are living now. And if I look over my life, I can find countless times when I have made assumptions about people with varying levels of accuracy. Being from the Midwest, I thought Californians were nuts and loons (that one might still be true). When I first started teaching, I was perplexed when I had Asian students who did poorly in class and in particular (gasp!) didn't do their homework. I assessed that store owner in Indiana was a "non-Amish" person taking advantage of the hard-working Amish quilters—even though I knew nothing about him personally.

To be fair, I have to give some grace to others when I am stereotyped or judged incorrectly because *I do it too*. In fact, Paul implies this need to be careful of our personal posture toward others in Romans 2:1. While he may not have stereotyping precisely in mind, he warns us about harshly judging others when we have similar sins in our own lives: "You, therefore, have no excuse, you who pass judgment on someone else, for at whatever point you judge another, you are condemning yourself, because you who pass judgment do the same things."

If I'm honest with myself, I have to admit that what I have accused some people of doing to me, I've done to others, just in different ways. This realization can have the interesting and convicting impact of short-circuiting my impulse to criticize and condemn those who stereotype me because I find the mirror turned around on myself. This has led me to ponder how this tendency reflects a human problem and not just a racial problem. It doesn't excuse horrible behavior, but I wonder if there is a real difference, or maybe a continuum, between an innocent human mistake and malicious intent.

While we can still criticize stereotyping, we should also honestly acknowledge that our compulsion to do it stems from a basic human limitation. Scientists have discovered that we humans not only like to generalize and categorize, but to a certain extent, we *must* do this. Our brains would otherwise be overwhelmed with information, paralyzing us with indecision if we weren't able to categorize. Assigning someone or something to a category based on a few key traits is necessary if we wish to live efficiently in the world. For example, my brain will tell me that while I do not need to be afraid of some furry creatures, such as golden retrievers, I very much need to be afraid of others, such as bears. And while I have never encountered a bear in person, I know that if I ever see one while hiking, I should not treat it like a pet. I definitely do not want to be the person feeding the bear sniffing at her foot. I found this warning posted at a ranger station, featuring a prebite picture of the bear's snout next to an unfortunate woman's foot, the sign presumably there to educate others who were tempted to make a similar categorization error.

We need to make some generalizations simply to function in the world. As Leonard Mlodinow describes, "Thinking in terms of generic categories such as 'bears,' 'chairs,' and 'erratic drivers' helps us to navigate our environment with great speed and efficiency; we understand an object's gross significance first and worry about its individuality later. Categorization is one of the most important mental acts we perform, and we do it all the time."[2] This means that in some sense we must categorize. The greater issue seems to be how we use these categories, particularly when we categorize people. For example, what happens when we continue to treat people based on broad categories and never get around to the individuality Mlodinow talks about, or we simply refuse to see it?

A few years back, my husband and I went out for lunch with a small group of people from our church. The group included our pastor and that week's guest speaker.

As the guest speaker was a seminary professor, my pastor introduced me as a seminary professor as well. The speaker's response to this information was to tell me that his assistant was Korean, and for the rest of the lunch the only time he would talk to me was to tell me how great his Korean assistant was and how much he and his wife were looking forward to going to Korea and having her show them around the country. Nothing was said about my being a professor. No questions asked about what I taught. There was no Christian academic "shop talk," as normally happens when I meet a fellow professor. Only gushing praise about his Korean assistant. I probably had less in common with his assistant than with him, at least culturally, since she was a native Korean and I had grown up in America, whereas he and I had spent decades in the same profession and in the same country. But he responded as if his Korean assistant was our primary—almost the only—point of connection.

Most of the time, I don't mind when I meet someone for the first time and they make assumptions about me. Again, since I do the same thing, I have little grounds for judgment. Getting to know people is all about going *beyond* the surface stuff to find out who they really are. But I am likely to bristle when someone hangs on to a rigid stereotype or an assumption rather than trying to see me for who I am. I don't like it when I feel like they are not interested in relating to me as a person, but rather as a category. My friend David may have a disability, but he is much, much more than a "blind person." And while he certainly appreciates that people want to pray for him, wanting someone to get to know him first sounds reasonable to me.

Here is the tension we all must learn to navigate. We need to categorize, but there are problems caused by generalizing—especially about other people. We naturally resist being categorized by our external characteristics before someone has a chance to "know" us. We don't want to be known superficially or, worse, to be told who we are when we believe we are something different. We want people to see us with depth and complexity rather than through stereotypical assumptions. We want to be seen as real people, not conglomerations of characteristics that may or may not apply to us.

But since we cannot avoid all generalizing, or perhaps even stereotyping to a certain degree, what are we to do? Mlodinow suggests a way forward: "The challenge is not how to stop categorizing but how to become aware when we do it in ways that prevent us from being able to see individual people for who they are."[3] One simple thing I have found helpful is to change my assumptions once I realize they are incorrect. Like generalizing, making assumptions is something we do all the time. But here is where we can learn and grow: we need to be willing to change when new information causes us to question our assumptions.

When I step into an elevator, I generally assume it will take me safely to my destination. I don't feel the need to read and verify the latest safety inspection or watch it go up and down successfully a couple times before getting on it myself. However, on the day I stepped into the office elevator, pressed the button, and the lights went out, I immediately modified my assumptions about the reliability of that elevator! This change in my thinking compelled me to make a quick dash through the doors before they closed, thereby saving me from a potentially unpleasant fate.

Even though I am a racial minority, I have to admit that I sometimes have stereotypes about other minorities. A Hispanic friend and colleague wrote an article where he talked about how his children were treated as "foreigners" even though they were born in the United States.[4] I had assumed for so long that feeling like a foreigner was part of my uniquely Asian experience that it hadn't occurred to me that others, like my friend, could feel the same way. I realized that my view of my colleague was limited and needed to change. And this is only one example of how I have found a need to correct my views—and one of the most benign.

If the reality of the situation is that God has created us so we cannot function in the world without some type of generalizing, even stereotyping, then we have to begin there. Our shortcomings will inevitably lead to misunderstandings. Sometimes our views will be hurtful without our even realizing it. Sometimes they are malicious. At other times they are not. But they all contribute to the problem of living separately and divided, apart from one another.

As members of Christ's body, we are different, yet we are one. I find this truth easy to say, but much, much more difficult to live out. I suspect that most of us believe the same thing. Our differences and limitations provide infinite opportunities for misunderstanding, and when sin overtakes us, we descend into objectification, condescension, bitterness, and hatred of one another.

Paul knew firsthand how these obstacles plagued the Christian community. They were there from the start. But he also believed Christ could overcome them. In the kingdom of God, ethnic differences and tensions are opportunities for the transformative power of the gospel to be put on display to a watching world. In the world, differences often lead to conflict, even violence. But in the Spirit-led community, the oneness of believers is a testament to the power of the One who saves them.

CHAPTER 8

DIFFERENT BY DESIGN

As difficult as our current problems seem, they are not all that unique. Being able to unify hostile ethnic groups was a major problem for the new Christian community. But the potential for oneness was a central promise and characteristic of the gospel. The idea that these groups could live in harmony, and even more—actually love one another—was far beyond the imagination of the first-century mind. For Paul it is part of the "mystery" of Christ (Eph. 3:3–6).[1] This mystery could only be known by God's revelation.

I have always been fascinated by optical illusions, such as those crazy-making M. C. Escher drawings, where you follow the person walking up the stairs only to discover the stairs lead down to the basement, or the Magic Eye images, which look like colorful fuzz or a bad Monet painting until you focus (or unfocus) your eyes correctly and are rewarded with a hidden image protruding 3D-like from the page.

I love optical illusions because they remind me that there is more to see than what I perceive. If I learn to look in a different way, I can find something new, something that was always there but that I couldn't perceive at first.

I had a colleague once tell me, "Evangelicals love Paul because he tells us what to do." True enough. But doesn't Paul also tell us how to think? And by this, I don't mean what to think as much as *how* to view something, a new way of seeing, a different perspective from my straightforward, Westernized, twenty-first-century frame of mind. If Paul and the rest of the New Testament writers show me how to see, perhaps one of these ways of seeing has something to say about today's racial differences.

In Galatians 3:28, Paul says something truly remarkable. He declares that there is "neither Jew nor Gentile," but they are "one." This passage has received more than its fair share of ink over the years, particularly because Paul also says there is neither male nor female. But Paul's statement about the two ethnic groups is no less astounding. He seems to speak to a transcendent reality, implying the irrelevance of traditional distinctions. It doesn't matter if you are Jew or gentile! There is something bigger than ethnic differences because what really matters is being in Christ.

At first glance it appears that with this statement the significance of ethnic differences has, for all intents and purposes, been abolished, and we should be what some call "color blind." But this view creates tension with something Paul says elsewhere. In other places, he is quite insistent about the continuing relevance of these distinctions. For example, in Romans 1:16, Paul speaks about the universality of gospel, saying it is "the power of God for salvation to everyone who believes" and then follows up with "first to the Jew, then to the Gentile." Some have suggested this means Jews get the first crack at salvation. Others argue it means Jews are more important in some sense. Whichever one it is, the sense of Jewish priority continues in the rest of the epistle. Paul goes on to say, for example, "What advantage, then, is there in being a Jew . . . ? Much in every way!" (Rom. 3:1–2). Interestingly, for us gentiles who might be a little put off by these Jewish privileges, Paul says that this honored place also comes with a distinct downside, which is that Jews also get priority for "tribulation and distress" (Rom. 2:9). The book of Romans is filled with these types of Jew-gentile distinctions (e.g., 2:10; 3:1–2; 11:1–32), which makes it very difficult to hold that those ethnic identities are no longer relevant.

Here's the conundrum. While saying there is neither Jew nor gentile, Paul simultaneously seems to think there is very much still a Jew and gentile category, and that both of these sentiments still matter in some way. Being Jewish or gentile was both irrelevant and supremely relevant. How in the world can he think that? And if these ethnic distinctions persist, what does it mean for us today?

The neither/nor part of Paul's statement seems fairly straightforward. In Christ we can all be accepted into the family of God. We share a common identity and a common salvation in Christ. The barriers that previously separated people—those related to race, gender, and status—have been torn down.[2] But as for such distinctions, the early church did not try to overlook or abolish these particular ethnic identities. On the contrary, they let Jews be Jews and gentiles be gentiles. The important application of this truth became how they could live together and love one another *as* Jews and gentiles. Christ was calling the new community to "group-transcending values,"[3] which allowed them to keep their particular cultural identities even as they lived according to the larger values of the kingdom of God.

I find I need to let that thought sink in for a little while. These early followers of Jesus were members of the new Christian movement, but they could still be Christians as Jews or as gentiles. Paul didn't proclaim a single overarching "Christian" identity that negated their cultural identities. What held them together was their shared values and love of Christ as members of the family of God. But they were united *as* Jews and gentiles. In fact, their oneness *as* Jew and gentile seems to be one of the key parts of their Christian unity.

Paul tells us more about the profound implications of their unity in Christ *as* Jew and gentile. When he speaks of the inclusion of gentiles into the body of Christ with the Jews as the "mystery of Christ" (Eph. 3:3–6), he is hardly saying their differences are now irrelevant. Rather, the point is that God has brought the two together. There is now to be reconciliation and peace. Their new identity as being one directly impacts their relationships with one another.

An obstacle to that oneness was the significant social tension and clash of cultures in the new Christian movement as the two groups attempted to live together. A notable instance of this occurs in Acts 15:5–11, where we read about something called the Jerusalem Council. Although all were saved in Christ, the church wondered whether the gentiles who had become members of this new movement, a movement that grew out of Judaism, still had to keep the Mosaic law and be circumcised, which was the mark of the covenant for the Jews. In the end the council decided that neither keeping the Mosaic law nor circumcision was necessary, and the gentiles only needed to "abstain from what has been sacrificed to idols, and from blood, and from what has been strangled, and from sexual immorality" (Acts 15:29 ESV). The upshot of this was that the gentiles could become Christ followers without having to become Jewish proselytes and follow the traditions that made one culturally Jewish. In other words, they could become equally part of the Christian movement while remaining distinctively gentile.[4]

On the other side, Paul affirmed the right of the Jewish Christians to remain Jewish when that came into question. In Romans 14–15 we see a dispute in the church that appears to be a conflict between Jewish believers who want to keep parts of the food laws and gentile believers who see them as obsolete. This is an especially fascinating passage that we'll return to later, but for now we can simply notice that Paul upholds the rights of the Jewish believers to keep the food laws, even though he does not consider them a necessary part of the faith. In other words, he's letting them continue to be Jews, to be who they are. Paul himself never stopped personally identifying as an ethnic Israelite. He calls the other Jews his "brothers" (Acts 22:1; 23:1, 5, 6; 28:17) and his "people" (Acts 24:17; 28:19).[5] He nested his own identification as a Jew in his larger and newer identity as a follower of Jesus, but he did not stop being a Jew.[6]

What we see is a movement that thought it was vital to maintain ethnic distinctions, and that the believers could—and should—worship God while still being Jew and gentile. Even in their greater unity in Christ, their cultural differences mattered. But while the early church did not ask anyone to leave behind their Jewish or gentile identities, profound relational obstacles still threatened their unity. Somehow, in retaining ethnic identities, they had to not only get along but also learn to be in community with and love one another.

This may be something we need to pay a bit more attention to as we wrestle with the relational obstacles to our unity as different races. How do we honor the uniqueness of different people and racial groups while also living according to larger kingdom beliefs such as our unity in Christ? Perhaps even more, what is the point of God making us one while preserving our distinctiveness? Is there a unique way the gospel makes itself known by having such different people, with all their special challenges, learn to love one another?

Paul's declaration of the establishment of peace between Jews and gentiles is especially remarkable because he is fully aware of their preexisting hostility. In

Paul's day the two groups were characterized by mutual animosity. Jewish hatred was fueled by their long history of being oppressed by gentiles. Jewish laws prohibiting eating with or marrying gentiles led to Jewish contempt for gentiles, which in turn fostered gentile hatred and suspicion of the Jews.[7] As these dynamics endured for generations, it is not difficult to imagine how deep seated and intractable those feelings and beliefs were. Often, these differences were enough to incite hatred against someone just for being Jewish or gentile. In the midst of these long-standing hostilities, Paul now declares that Christ, the one who died for them, not only broke down the dividing wall but replaced animosity and estrangement with love for one another as fellow members of his body (Eph. 4:16).

Their unity was not supposed to deny their distinctions. It was Jews being able to love gentiles *as gentiles*, and gentiles being able to love Jews *as Jews*, with all the history and baggage on both sides. This is what made their oneness so remarkable. And we see this specifically play out in the New Testament.[8]

When we see the coming together of Jew and gentile in the early church, we see the Christian community testifying to the work of God by living out "the unity of the Spirit in the bond of peace" (Eph. 4:3 ESV). Rather than traditional animosity and suspicion, their unity was about the way they related to and treated one another, "with all humility and gentleness, with patience bearing with one another in love" (Eph. 4:2 ESV). Instead of the cultural and ethnic distinctions causing discord, we see the unified worship of God *as* different peoples, something only possible as transformed followers of the crucified Christ.

For us today, we may be neither Black nor White, Asian nor Hispanic, and at the same time we are very much Black and White, Asian and Hispanic, all one in Christ. Our unity is composed of very human differences, differences that matter and yet are integral aspects of a oneness that uniquely reflects our Savior. This is who we are, and it is our calling to live out.

⇁≀⇀

But this living out has its own particular challenges that relate to our being human.

Someone once said to me, "When I look at you, I don't see someone who is Asian." Perhaps that person meant that my being Asian really doesn't matter in terms of how she relates to me. I understand the sentiment. I don't want people to see me simply as Asian. My day-to-day identity is made up of many different aspects: I am a woman, wife, daughter, grandmother, scholar, dog lover, and so forth. Being Asian is relevant in some contexts, less relevant in others.

However, something is odd about that particular expression. I found myself thinking, "How can you *not* see me as Asian? When I look in the mirror, *I* see someone Asian." It seems pretty hard to miss that fact if you're looking at me. Sometimes people have the faulty idea that we shouldn't think about race unless we're talking about our unity as fellow members of the human race.

This seems to be what's behind the "color blind" idea, but it misses a crucial part of what it means to be human in the world.

For Paul the difficulty of uniting Jews and gentiles was that they had already lived as Jews and gentiles. After they began following Christ, they didn't stop being Jewish or gentile, nor were they supposed to. Similarly, we all live with various experiences that impact how we view the world and how we see ourselves and others. The impressions they leave on us don't go away once we are in Christ.

Let's consider one aspect of my particular being in the world, which is the fact that I am short. More precisely, I am 5'3", or as I like to say, 5'3 1/2", because when you're short, even a half-inch matters. My height may not impact my worth in Christ, but it makes a difference in my daily experience. I can get into small spaces that my 6'5" husband cannot (he also does not feel the need to include fractional inches when stating his height). He can reach things on shelves that I cannot. When I first started teaching, all of my department colleagues were over six feet tall, and standing with them made me feel like a small shrub in the middle of a forest of tall trees.

Recently, I was standing on a stepstool holding up a bathroom light while my husband screwed it in. For a brief moment, I stood slightly taller than him. I found this vantage point quite interesting. I felt rather powerful to be looking down at someone, a most unusual experience for me. It made me wonder what it would be like if I experienced life like this all the time.

I caught a glimpse of this reality when my husband was involved in an incident with an angry young man. The young man was driving recklessly and almost hit a car coming out of our church driveway. The incident came to a head when he stormed out of his car, yelling as he approached us. My husband pulled his 6'5" frame out of our car in response. When the young man got a glimpse of my very tall husband, he came to an immediate stop, and with a look of shock on his face shouted, "Are you kidding me?" He practically fell over himself as he scrambled back into his car as fast as he could and drove away.

Needless to say, no one has responded to me that way. The only "Are you kidding me?" comment I've received came when I was a baby-faced first-year seminary student, and I introduced myself to some freshman college students as the teaching assistant. My husband and I may live in the same house and do many of the same things, but in some ways we live in very different worlds.

We all have a multitude of physical characteristics that make a difference in how people respond to us and how we experience the world. A more serious example of this is the difference being a woman can make in how safe I feel in certain situations. When I was a full-time professor teaching on campus, only my female colleagues and I would talk about how we don't like to walk in certain areas of the campus by ourselves at night, or why we don't want to be the last person in the building after dark. In those situations we would call Campus Safety, have a husband or boyfriend meet us, or simply go home early. Maybe we were being overly cautious, but it was still something we believed we had to consider. I never heard a male colleague talk about it.

In a similar way, my race impacts how I experience some situations. When my husband and I were thinking of moving to Nashville, we spent some time hanging out in some of the smaller towns around the city. We went to one such town and had lunch at a cute outdoor café at the town center. In the middle of this area was a statue, and after lunch we went over to look at it. It was a statue of a Confederate soldier.

This was right around the time of the first explosion of calls to tear down Confederate monuments. As we gazed at the statue, commemorating the soldier's devotion to the cause, I tried to take what I considered a responsible, rational approach by considering the various arguments I had heard for not taking them down. I tried to impartially assess the arguments as best I could. But I also found that just because you try to look at something in a rational way, it doesn't mean those feelings you have aren't present. Nor does it mean those feelings are irrelevant. After a little while, I decided to simply consider for that moment how I *felt* about the statue. And what came to me was this: "Looking at this statue makes me feel icky."

Icky because it brought back feelings I had growing up in that northern Minnesota town, feelings that surfaced again for me with surprising ease. I began to wonder if we moved here if I would have to relive those same emotions all over again. As an adult with a lifetime of experiences and perspective, I have the ability to see things differently than I did as a child just by learning more about the world. But at the same time, those experiences are a part of my life, which has been lived in this body, and they occurred at a very formative time. It would be naïve to think their impact would just disappear. I found myself thinking about experiences and feeling emotions I hadn't dealt with in years, and for the rest of the week I became obsessed with spotting other Asians so I could better discern if I would be out of place in this new area. (I found four.) Most of all, I just felt tired.

Perhaps I am making a big deal out of something trivial. Or maybe not. My previous experience led me to look at our potential move in a certain way. And although so far our move has turned out far more positively than I had expected, it does not change the fact that we are all shaped by our interactions with our environment, and those interactions are profoundly influenced by the way God has made us in our bodies. Evangelicals tend to be better at thinking about "spiritual" matters and not as good at understanding what it means to live in the body. We talk a lot about going to heaven, but I hear less about how our destiny is to live in resurrected bodies. Even our language about saving souls is an indication of how we can overlook our bodies when thinking about our salvation.[9] However, "human embodiment—life in a physical, material body—is the proper state of human existence."[10]

Philosopher Dallas Willard talked about how our failure to think correctly about the body resulted in distancing our faith from daily human life.[11] We focus so much on things like the forgiveness of sins that we don't think about new life in Christ as involving "the concrete, embodied existence of our human personalities walking with Jesus in his easy yoke."[12] But we need to think about life in the body. Susan Grove Eastman writes, "Our bodies are interacting with our environments from the very beginning, all the time, and this interaction profoundly shapes the development of the self in interpersonal ways."[13] We are shaped by what happens in the body. Our identity is not individuals isolated in protective bubbles. We interact with our environments and are changed by them.[14] My core identity may be "in Christ" like everyone else's, but I live a particular life of "in Christness" that is uniquely my own. This unique life includes many facets: being a woman, short, bespectacled, and Korean. We *are* Jew and gentile, and at the same time we are *neither* Jew nor gentile.

Our unity necessarily and fundamentally involves our varied lives in the body—both our own bodies and the body of Christ. We share the same Spirit and the same humanity, and yet our experience of life is inevitably and radically different from each other. We are all unique, yet we are all integrated into the multifaceted body of Christ. We are different and one at the same time.

A couple years ago, I heard a sermon in which the pastor pointed out something I had never thought about before but in hindsight seems incredibly obvious. In Acts 2, the Spirit comes upon the believers at Pentecost. When they begin speaking to the crowd, everyone hears them *in their own language*. The Spirit doesn't translate what they say, nor does the crowd receive a special ability to understand a spiritual language. Instead, the Spirit takes what the believers say, spoken in one language, and miraculously allows people to hear it in their own tongue.

This is a testimony to the Spirit's affirmation of cultural identity. It is even more remarkable when one realizes that doing so was completely unnecessary. While they could have had different countries of origin, as members of the Jewish Diaspora, the crowd would have been fluent in Hebrew/Aramaic or Greek, and perhaps both.[15] I had imagined a bunch of people wandering around Jerusalem speaking different languages, a somewhat chaotic scene like a first-century tower of Babel, but more likely they all would have been able to communicate with each other just fine.[16] When the Spirit chooses to have them hear the disciples in their own languages, it is not needed from a practical standpoint. But it affirms that although they are all Jews, God chooses to honor where they are from as reflected in their differing languages. Their inclusion does not demand one common culture. But it is real unity, a unity of the Spirit.[17]

Perhaps the point of the Spirit's action is to show that God's unity is far more than bland uniformity. Perhaps the point is that what binds us together is more profound than common characteristics or shared ideas, and we should not be satisfied with flighty and superficial bonds. God's unity transforms enemies into friends, and even more.

In Romans 5:1–11, Paul says something amazing: we have God's love poured into our hearts through the Spirit.

What is this incredible love? Simply this, that Christ died for those who did not deserve it. He died for those who were God's enemies.

Enemies. What a thought! God's work of reconciliation seems the opposite of what we see today, where anyone who disagrees with us can become our "enemy" and definitely not someone worthy of our love and sacrifice. But God's means of reconciliation was to die for us while we were his enemies. And this was the love the members of the Christian community, who had been enemies with each other, were to demonstrate to one another. It was not just trying to get along, saying the "right" things, or rectifying all wrongs. It was a cross-shaped humility that produced genuine love and concern for others. It was to be practiced by everyone, for it would not work if only some did it, because all were called to be like Christ. It was more powerful than anything the world could come up with, whether Rome's armies or long-standing ethnic hatreds, and it was only possible through submission to Christ and his kingdom and the life-changing work of the Spirit.

CHAPTER 9

CALLED TO LIVE TOGETHER

So how do we live in this mystery, the mystery of living together "in Christ," in these limited, fragile, and fallen human bodies? It should come as no surprise that we do not do this very well.

When I was in the fifth grade, I had a rare moment of inspiration. I decided to start a club. With my tendency for literalness evident even at that tender age, I appropriately dubbed it the "Fun Club." There were three charter (and ultimately only) members of my club: myself and two friends. The primary goal of the club was, not surprisingly, to have fun. I don't recall what we actually did that was fun, except having the satisfaction of being part of an exclusive group dedicated to this noble goal.

I didn't think to ask why it seemed so important to have a club for this purpose since three eleven-year-olds should be able to come up with ways to enjoy their time without having to make it so official. But somehow, being a part of this group gave us more incentive to plan activities. It also made us feel special, as we were all part of a group in which no one else was included. *We* were the Fun Club, and other people were not.

What we discovered was not so different from what other kids our age already knew. Belonging to a group gives you an identity. It is an important part of the way God has made us. But this also means a significant aspect of your identity can be defined by others who are not members of your group. That is part of the potential benefit and seductive danger of groups: the possibility of gaining something, but at the expense of others. As Yale law professor Amy Chua describes, "Humans are tribal. We need to belong to groups. We crave bonds and attachments. . . . But the tribal instinct is not just an instinct to belong. It is also an instinct to exclude."[1] The pain I felt growing up was made much worse by those who continually reminded me that I didn't belong, that I was left out. But the larger truth is that we do this to each other all the time.

This type of exclusion at the expense of others happened in the early church, as the new believers struggled to overcome long-standing prejudices. Paul and the other New Testament writers responded by giving those first Christians a vision for their new corporate life in Christ, a vision that is the same for us today.

In addition to "neither Jew nor Gentile," Galatians 3:28 mentions slave and free and male and female. In other words, it includes class (or more accurately in antiquity, status) and gender. The pairing "male and female" tends to get more attention because of its role in the gender debate, but as a whole what Paul is doing is presenting three very prominent pairs of opposites, pairs that generally represented the ways people were divided from each other at the time.[2] As one scholar describes it, these three pairs were "the source of the most bitter hostility and antagonisms."[3] This is Paul's way of saying unity applies to everyone and all groups, including and perhaps most of all those who are typically characterized by separation and conflict. Paul uses these illustrations to promote his broader point about how true unity is so incredibly difficult that it can only happen in the Spirit.

To better appreciate how hard this unity is, it helps to think about how easily we gravitate to the opposite. We don't need much prompting to divide, and those divisions are often characterized by antagonism toward others. As human beings, one of our most fundamental needs is to have meaning in our lives, and one way we get that meaning is by vying for supremacy. A group identity is not enough; we pit our identity against someone else's in an ongoing contest for validation and preeminence. In our desire to identify with a group, we want to see our group as set apart from and better than others. This can happen with any group, such as those based on race, class, or political beliefs or even those connected with hometown sports teams, clothing brands, or preferred coffee-making methods.

Just as we can easily find more ways to be divided than just our racial differences, so too could the early church. For example, 1 Corinthians 11:17–34 speaks about the Lord's Supper. In it, Paul warns against taking the cup and the bread in an "unworthy" manner (v. 27). I have heard various understandings of what constitutes an "unworthy" manner, such as taking communion when one still has unconfessed sin in one's heart, when a person still has something against someone else, or when one is not yet a follower of Jesus. As good as it is to be careful of these things, Paul likely has something else in mind.

He doesn't tell the Corinthians to make sure they know Jesus or confess hidden sin. Something else was going on in Corinth. Paul chastises some of them for getting "drunk" while others are hungry. He scolds the one who would go ahead "with your own private suppers" (11:21). Something is happening in the way the Corinthians relate to one another, and the problem is that some "humiliate those who have nothing," with the implication that they "despise the church of God" (11:22).

The situation is easily overlooked because we tend to envision the Lord's Supper happening according to the way we take it in our own churches. We drink grape juice from little plastic cups and eat tiny pieces of crackers. We all take the same elements, and we sit quietly in our seats and ponder the impact of Christ in our lives.

But there were some critical differences in the way the early church took the Lord's Supper, and those give us clues as to what the Corinthians' problem was. For the first believers, the Lord's Supper was part of a larger meal. When you ate meals in antiquity, it was common for the rich and powerful to have a prominent place and to discriminate against the poor. If the church met in the house of a wealthy patron, that person got to decide where everyone ate. Not surprisingly the favored guests would likely eat in the smaller dining area called the triclinium, while everyone else would be relegated to the second-class accommodations in the atrium.[4] The host might serve better or larger quantities of food to the high-status guests.[5] On other occasions, the meal could be what was called a "basket dinner," where each person would bring their own dinner in a basket. Unlike our contemporary church potlucks where everyone contributes a dish to share so everyone has a full meal, sharing was not the norm, and one person might bring a bountiful feast for themselves, while another might have little.[6]

All of this was common practice in that culture. It was nothing unique to the church. They were simply doing what everyone else did in showcasing and giving better treatment to those who were the "haves," while making clear who were the "have nots." But Paul says that whether or not this is normal in the larger culture, by no means should they do this in the church.[7] In the worshiping community, which is Christ's body, they "proclaim the Lord's death" (11:26) through the supper. By celebrating this in a way that shows some are more favored than others, they are making the Lord's Supper mean something very different. As a result, Paul scolds them: "It is not the Lord's Supper you eat" (11:20). When they are humiliating those who are already lacking, how can this be something that honors the one who died for them (11:22)? The gathered church is meant to reflect Christ's humility rather than vie for personal superiority.

The Corinthians were using the supper to proclaim some as better than others. But they were merely doing what people throughout the ages have done, just in their own cultural ways. In their desire to gain, show, and reinforce their supremacy, they were not much different than we are. In *Subliminal: How Your Unconscious Mind Rules Your Behavior,* Leonard Mlodinow explains that (1) human beings naturally want to belong to a group as distinguished from other groups, and (2) we want to be in a group that proclaims superiority over other groups. As he says, "We are highly invested in feeling different from one another—and superior—no matter how flimsy the grounds for our sense of superiority."[8] Wanting to make ourselves look and feel better than others comes quite naturally to us.

If we look carefully, we can begin to see how hierarchies are used everywhere to make ourselves feel better and how this can harm others. My family faced challenges as Asians in an all-White community, but that was hardly the only hierarchy in my town, and not even the only ethnic hierarchy. We had an elderly neighbor who complained to me one day about how she was discriminated against when she was in high school because she was Finnish. I wanted to shout, "Finnish! Are you *kidding* me?" But I knew she was serious because a dark bitterness came over her normally cheerful demeanor when she told me. A friend later explained to me that in the old days some people saw Finns as being at the bottom of the Scandinavian hierarchy, and she had probably had a very difficult time when she was younger. There is a general human tendency to position ourselves as better than others and to abuse those who are lower on the hierarchy. In earlier years in the very Scandinavian town of my childhood, even Finns were a target of abuse.[9]

We need to think more deeply about what motivates us and causes these divisions as well as the problems that come along with them. Paul doesn't condemn Jew or gentile for identifying as such. He objects to what they do with their racial identity. Whereas human differences often lead to conflict and hurt, in the kingdom of God differences are the means whereby we express a transcendent love. Ironically, these differences make this possible. We are called to love someone who is not like us, who in our natural human state we would see as "other," someone we cannot entirely relate to. Rather than vie for superiority based on our various identities or ignore the pain or difficulties these differences have caused, we are called to set aside our desire to see ourselves and our perspective as supreme. We die to ourselves so we can see the other person for who they are.

We are not to think of ourselves more highly than we ought (Rom. 12:3), but to consider others as better than ourselves (Phil. 2:3). We should care for each other in our differences rather than use them against one another. This is because we are one in Christ.

As part of this care, 1 Corinthians 12:26 talks about suffering together with a suffering member. I hear this a lot in diversity talks, and it is important. We are to be here for one another, as one member's pain impacts the whole body.

But there is something else we must consider to get a more complete picture. I hear much less about rejoicing together when one member of the body is honored, which is the other half of that verse. Paul describes both the suffering together and the rejoicing together as having "equal concern" for one another (12:25). The point is that all of us are to care for one another, which might look different for each of us and may change with time and circumstance. This applies to all who are members of Christ. All who belong to the one body. All care for all. Our role as the community is to discern what kind of care each member needs.

The insidiousness of sin tempts us to leverage our differences for destructive ends, to gain power over others and for ourselves. In their abuse of the poor, the rich Corinthians were sending a far different message than a proclamation of Jesus's death, the ultimate act of humility. Paul explains in Philippians that a key aspect of Jesus's humility was his willingness to not use his status of being God and instead descend to the lowest human level by becoming a slave (Phil. 2:6–11). Rather than proclaim superiority, even his rightful superiority, he took on inferiority. He did the opposite of what we naturally want to do. And what higher position can one claim than being God? If Jesus could give up those privileges and take the humiliating status of a slave, it seems utterly foolish to seek our own meager status claims in this world.

Focusing exclusively on our commonality is a denial

of our unique, individual bodily existence. We run the danger of not seeing people as they truly are. Yet focusing only on our differences obscures the reality of our oneness, making us vulnerable to the very human impulse to seek dominance over others. What's the alternative? Being united as Jew and gentile in the body of Christ. This is how we consider the way God has made us as individuals while at the same time we learn to live together as those who are "one," who through the Spirit grow in unity as we follow the example of our crucified Lord.

⟱

When my husband and I first started dating, I learned something important about him. I had seen those TV commercials portraying the doofus White husband who always has to be saved from his stupidity and incompetence by his amazingly talented multitasking wife or his wise-beyond-their-years teenage children. Even the family dog always seems to know more about what is going on. I never really thought about what it would be like to be a middle-aged White male watching those commercials. As my husband and I got to know each other, I learned to appreciate that just as my experiences as an Asian female impact how I view the world, the same was true for him as a White male. I discovered that being willing to understand his story didn't diminish or invalidate my own. Even more importantly, I learned that being so focused on myself and my vantage point often made it impossible for me to see him as a real person.

I want to be seen, but I must also be willing to see

others. It is a challenge to step outside of ourselves, wherever we are, to stop being the center of our own universe. This is excruciatingly hard to do, particularly as psychologists have identified our society today as increasingly narcissistic and less empathetic.[10] This step is necessary, however, because it is the only way we can ever truly see the other person.

Of course, no one can completely know and relate to another, and we must recognize and accept that limitation. But perhaps that is part of the process—the story of the grace we are to give one another—to love in imperfect understanding when we are dealing with our own broken lives. How else could Jew and gentile confront the challenges of loving those they could not relate to naturally? How would they overcome their mutual suspicion, hostility, and hatred, festering and nurtured over generations, and now handed down to their children and their children's children like precious family heirlooms?

Since only God can know us fully, our lives with each other will inevitably be characterized by limitation, misunderstanding, and unknowing. Throw in sinful inclinations like jealousy, suspicion, hatred, and the need to dominate, and you have an extremely volatile situation.

If our natural tendency is indeed to divide, strive for superiority, and war with one another, then the oneness of the church becomes all the more incredible. Being the same is easy. Conformity comes naturally. To be aware of the differences, including all of the pain and confusion they have caused, and then to be able to love each other is indeed more than we can do on our own. It can only be done through God's grace and the Spirit's power. It is dying to self as the center of the universe and embracing the only perspective that can make things right.

As I reflect on my childhood and those Barbie dolls, I see that having a doll who looked like me might have affirmed me as an individual, but it could not fix a more fundamental problem: *How do I relate to people who are not like me?* A Korean Barbie could not teach me how to live with people who have different skin color, gender, talents, tastes, interests, and backgrounds.

As important as it was to be validated for who I am, I needed to go beyond personal validation. The point of life in the world is not for everyone else to affirm me in all my uniqueness. If anything, it seems rather self-centered to expect everyone to understand how *I* feel. The world doesn't revolve around me, as much as I might wish that were true.

Instead, it is necessary to hold some things in tension. We must acknowledge real differences and the difficulties they may cause. But we must also see our real unity and potential to live in oneness based on our commonality in Christ and as his body. In him our racial group identities matter profoundly and yet are encompassed within an even greater identity. We all have different aspects of our identity, and our union in Christ both transcends and preserves those distinctions. We become transformed gentiles and transformed Jews in the Spirit-created body of Christ.[11] To be able to live in this truth and love each other, in all our weaknesses and fallibility, through Christ who lives in us and loves us, is both our challenge and our promise from God.

CHAPTER 10

ACKNOWLEDGING

OUR LIMITATIONS

One of the most cringe-inducing events for many Asian Americans is the dreaded question.

"So where are you from?"

In my experience, the exchange generally goes something like this:

> **Well-intentioned person:** So where are you from?
>
> **Me:** I'm from Southern California.
>
> **Well-intentioned person:** No, I mean, where are you *from*?
>
> **Me:** I live in Yorba Linda, which is in Orange County, just outside of Los Angeles, and near Disneyland.
>
> **Well-intentioned person:** No, no. Where are you *from*?

Me: Well . . . I grew up in a small town in
northern Minnesota, and then went to
college on the East Coast.

Well-intentioned person: (*Voice rising,
speaking more slowly to enunciate words
more clearly since it appears that I did not
understand what they are saying.*) No! I
mean . . . WHERE . . . ARE . . . YOU . . . FROMMMM?

Me: (*Sighing.*) My parents were born in Korea.

Well-intentioned person: I thought you were
Chinese.

These kinds of conversations were always particularly difficult for my mother. For her, they were constant reminders that she was not really seen as an American, despite the fact that she had left her homeland decades earlier, considered the United States to be her country, and was now a US citizen. These types of exchanges left her feeling that she would always be seen as a foreigner. She wouldn't be entirely rejected, but she would never be seen as belonging in the same way as everyone else.

My mother's hope was that at least her children would be viewed as Americans, and she continually affirmed our Americanness to us. When I was about five years old, after yet another "So where are you from?" exchange, my mother pulled me aside and said to me, "Don't let anyone tell you that you aren't an American. You were born here. You're 100 percent American."

I took that to heart. The next time I was out with

Mom and a man came up to us and asked me the question, I stood up straight and proudly proclaimed, "I'm 100 percent American!" I'm not sure what kind of response I expected, but the reaction I got was a loud and hearty laugh from the man. This, of course, threw me into confusion. Wasn't what I said the truth? If so, why would he laugh about it? My confusion was compounded when my mother, looking very embarrassed, quickly whisked me away. I didn't know what I had gotten wrong.

Perhaps part of that man's response came from the amusing sight of a little girl militantly asserting her national identity. Perhaps part of it was from getting an unexpected response to his question, since he was clearly anticipating something else. Incidents like these made me feel that while I might technically be an American, I was not seen as really American, at least not like my White classmates. Because of my ethnic background, I could not be "from" the United States, even though this was the only country I had ever known. Similar to my desire to be "normal," I was close but not quite enough to qualify for full membership. Besides, only a person whose Americanness was in doubt would feel the need to assert it like I had done. There was always something lacking that placed me permanently on the outside.

At the same time, I know that if I focus only on what happens to me, or my narrow point of view, I am missing an important part of the overall picture. I know I am as capable of misjudging and hurting as the next person. We all are. What are we supposed to do?

I am sensitive to my mother's feeling out of place, of being without a country that fully accepts her. It's not that my mother wouldn't be interested in talking about her homeland. It's more that for her the question highlights how she is not like everyone else, simply because of the way she looks. Too often she was a curiosity to be analyzed and studied, when she would rather be seen as a person with hopes, dreams, and fears, like all of us. Perhaps because of my protectiveness over my mother, I would get quite annoyed whenever people would ask her the question.

I was quite sure of my paradigm—that people who asked that question were some combination of clueless, insensitive, and/or racist—but there was an incident in my life that challenged my sense of personal moral superiority over those who dared to ask that offensive question. I was in grad school in Indiana, and a White friend and I decided to go shopping in a nearby town. We wandered into a store where the owner was not White, and my friend, always wanting to learn about new people and new cultures, walked up to him, and to my horror, asked, "So where are you from?"

In my mind's eye, I was instantly transported to a spot directly behind the man, where he could not see me but I could make frantic gestures to my friend—arms flailing, intensely shaking head, panicked look on my face—desperately signaling her to cease and desist. *Stop! Don't do this to him!*

However, to my utter surprise, the man was not offended at all. In fact, he was absolutely delighted that my friend had asked him the question. He said he had recently moved from Egypt and proceeded to regale her with stories of how wonderful his home country is. She was completely enraptured, which of course made him want to tell her more stories. This went on for about fifteen minutes, after which he told my friend what a wonderful person she was to be so interested in him, as opposed to all the other rude Americans who hadn't bothered to ask him where he was from.

I was speechless. The question that caused my mother so much distress was the same question this man wanted to be asked. Completely opposite reactions from two people who have very precise needs and desires—my mother to fit in and be accepted, and this man to be recognized for his uniqueness.

I realized that if I was someone who met my mother or this man, I had the capacity to help or harm them. The thought then occurred to me: *But how can you know?* If you have never met the person before, how do you know if asking the question will make the person experience the deep wounds of not fitting in, or if not asking the question will make the person feel unseen and unvalued?

The answer: *you can't know.*

In other words, if you've just met the person and don't already know them, it's likely impossible to know whether they want to be accepted and hate the reminders that they aren't, or whether they still identify so strongly with their country of origin that they want people in their new country to appreciate that.

Compounding the problem is that making the wrong choice can be extremely perilous. You can either be an insensitive, racist jerk who makes someone feel like they don't belong after they've risked their lives and sacrificed everything to bravely make their home in a strange new land, or you can be an insensitive, racist jerk who is so America-centric that you don't care one whit about anyone else's ethnic heritage if it refers to some inferior place outside of our hallowed shores. Given the negative downside (which kind of insensitive, racist jerk would you rather be?), it seems only human to take the easy way out by not saying anything because you don't want to be the problem or cause harm. We stay quiet because it seems safer to err with sins of omission, or we go in the opposite direction and proclaim a little too loudly our understanding and empathy so no one will miss our goodness.

All this has led me to an earth-shattering realization: there is no perfect solution to the conundrum. Or at least there is no solution in which we can be smart enough, clever enough, sensitive or enlightened enough that we can conduct our lives so flawlessly that no one will ever be hurt, offended, angry, defensive, or confused. In a world of profound differences where we lack the omniscience to know precisely what everyone's background is or why they react the way they do, we will always have those difficult, awkward, even painful moments if we are to truly live together. But this fits the gospel because the church's mission is not to expect omniscience and perfection but to somehow learn to live together even though we will inevitably, although not always intentionally, hurt or unfairly treat one another. In other words, we live not by rules but by relationships, and relationships are not easy to regulate since by definition they must be lived.

Furthermore, when we think about racial problems, we tend to focus on the most dramatic cases. But the smaller, daily experiences are also worthy of our attention since they too influence how we see ourselves and each other. They can separate us or even set us against one another. They pose their own challenges because it is harder to see their more subtle impact and cumulative effects.

One of the reasons I was so reluctant to move to Tennessee was because I loved living in Southern California. The ethnic diversity meant there were many restaurants, cultural events, and specialty shops to choose from. But I also appreciated the general atmosphere of differences reflected in the area's overall cultural quirkiness, such as when I went to my first concert and saw people dressed up in long gowns and tuxes standing next to others in shorts and sneakers. In Southern California there was a sense that you can be whoever you want to be, even if it's a little wacky.

In many ways I found LA to be comforting, particularly because of its racial makeup. I vividly remember my reaction stepping off the plane into the LAX terminal as I was finishing up grad school and interviewing for my first teaching position. This was before they renovated

LAX, so my first thought was, "This is a really dumpy airport for such a big city." However, after I got past that, my next thought was, "Wow, LA is so diverse." Taking in all of the White, Black, Hispanic, and Asian people in a normal place like an airport was almost a transcendent Toto-I-have-a-feeling-we're-not-in-Kansas-anymore moment for me. I had stepped into a completely new world, a world that instantly brought me a sense of comfort. I entered the mass of black-, brown-, and blond-haired people like a little kid stepping into a swimming pool on a hot summer day and feeling the pleasure of being engulfed in cool, comforting water. I didn't have to carry a continual sense of being different and knowing everyone else saw me as the odd one out. In that moment, I could forget about me.

I also realized how much I had been feeling a small but continual tension from my grad school years in Indiana. It was something I wasn't aware of until I experienced a distinct difference in LA: a palpable sense of relief. I would be among the first to say (understatement alert!) that LA has its share of problems, but the simple lesson SoCal taught me was that being able to relax is nice, and I really like that feeling. Being in a place where you don't fit is tiring, like having a low-grade fever all the time. It may not be enough to warrant an ER visit, but it exhausts you by its continual presence over days, months, and years, because you can never quite get away from it.

I know I'm not the only one who feels that way. In another air-travel-related event several years ago, I had an interesting conversation with a Hispanic woman on a plane. We started talking about how much we love LA, and the main reason was because it is so diverse. We both loved the variety of restaurants to choose from, and the freedom to be as dressy or casual as you want. But mostly, we liked the racial makeup . . . again, because we felt we could relax.

We talked about Tennessee, and I explained my hesitation to move there. I qualified my thoughts by saying I presumed a place like Nashville would likely be quite different than other areas. She agreed and shared a story. Once, she had gone to a particular spot in Tennessee, and the people there kept staring at her, as if they had never met anyone who was Hispanic before. We both agreed we were happy to be flying back to Southern California.

At that time I found myself reluctant to leave my life in California because I liked being able to relax and escape the tension of being different. Of course, this was another instance of my making blanket assumptions about Tennessee, as well as California, where I have had many friends there tell me about their own uncomfortable encounters. But the larger point is that it wasn't until I thought of moving away that I realized Southern California had been a haven of sorts for me. It was not something I wanted to give up, since I had now discovered how much that mattered to me.

～⁂～

Some people might consider my desire to be in a place like LA a rather trivial matter, but it reflects how important it is for us to feel accepted by others, to be a part of the group. This desire is not something we can turn on and off. It is a basic part of who we are. We were created to belong, and this desire entails how we are considered by others. This does not mean we have to be perfectly understood, as only God can do that, but it does show that we want to be valued and seen, even when we are not completely known.

In Ephesians 2:14 Paul talks about the peace that God has established between Jew and gentile. *Peace* in the biblical sense means more than an absence of a negative, as in no more hostility. We have something positive as well, as the Greek word for peace translates the Hebrew *shalom*, which communicates more a sense of well-being. Peace is a well-being that permeates both the individual and society and includes an element of justice.[1]

This peace entails more than an attitude and even more than an action. It is a reality we live out.[2] It takes place in real time, with real people, in real circumstances. It's easy to think that the racial situation we have in America and in our American churches is unique, that we are the only people in history who have had to deal with these kinds of problems. In some important ways, that is true. Every country and every Christian community face particular challenges. But I also suspect, as a very wise person once said, "There is nothing new under the sun."[3] In other words, while the specifics might be different, underneath it all, people don't change that much. All societies share the same sinful tendencies, including an inability to really get along and a driving propensity to segment, discriminate, abuse, and more. The challenge for the church then as now was how to unify a group of people who had a history of conflict, competition, suspicion, and worse into a community where the members truly loved one another.[4]

The challenge for the ancient church was how to unite ethnic Jews and gentiles, two groups separated by longstanding hostilities. When they became followers of Christ, however, they were called not only to live with one another but to be willing to sacrifice or even die for the other. How in the world would they accomplish this?

I love that so much of the New Testament comes to us in the form of actual letters rather than academic treatises. Besides the fact that academic writing has the potential to be insufferably tedious and boring (even for academics!), these letters give us a precious window into real life conflicts in the first-century church. We get the nitty gritty as Paul confronts problems ranging from fraud to incestuous relationships to heresy. These problems cannot be fixed by simplistic slogans or sincere but vacuous platitudes. He has to get down and dirty with them sometimes, and he isn't satisfied with quick and easy solutions. One way Paul teaches the community to deal with many of their conflicts is to challenge them to reconsider how they think about their relationships with each other. Their corporate identity is to inform, confront, and in the end radically reorient how they think about themselves and treat one another, including what it means to love.

One particular example is in 1 Corinthians 14, where the issue is spiritual gifts, especially speaking in tongues.

Surprisingly, Paul grounds his response by telling the Corinthians that while speaking in tongues is desirable, there is a greater gift which they should pursue, which is prophecy (1 Cor. 14:1, 39).

Why would Paul say this? Not only would urging them to seek this "greater" gift feed their competitiveness, but it seems to fly directly in the face of his other exhortations to humility, to consider others as better than themselves (Phil. 2:3). The answer, I believe, lies in Paul's rationale for this higher ranking and what it means for the community in their new life in Christ.

The Greco-Roman world of the first century was built upon honor and status distinctions.[5] In this hierarchical world, the Corinthians' interest in which gift would bestow greater status would be perfectly natural and understandable. Paul's answer does not simply assess the gifts, but it shows how he sees the Christian faith as critiquing and transcending this competitive culture.

Paul says prophecy is the more desirable gift because prophets are able to speak to the entire congregation in a way that is intelligible to everyone. In contrast, the tongues speaker's conversation is between themselves and God since no one can understand them unless there is an interpreter (e.g., 1 Cor. 14:2, 5, 13, 27).[6] In other words, the ability of a particular spiritual manifestation to benefit the entire body is the basis for assessing its worth. But what is especially noteworthy about Paul's answer is the basis for understanding what a gift is worth, and how he sees this impacting the unity of the congregation.

Paul's assessment about the gifts' relative value would

be a surprise to the ancient Corinthians. Christians were not the only ones to claim to have divine revelation. The culture was filled with religions that worshiped a variety of deities and saw the supernatural as permeating their world. For the Corinthian believers who were used to living in this environment, speaking in tongues would actually be the more honorable gift than prophecy. Speaking in tongues would have been regarded as heavenly speech, whereas prophecy was more normal human speech, albeit still divinely influenced.[7] We may see this belief echoed in Paul's description of speaking in the tongues of angels in 1 Corinthians 13:1, and in 1 Corinthians 14:2, where he says that the tongues speaker speaks to God and not humans. Prophecy, on the other hand, while still valuable, was seen as mediated through the mind (1 Cor. 14:14, 19), so not as direct, and therefore less esteemed.

However, Paul comes to the opposite conclusion. Prophecy, not tongues, is now the more valuable gift. It is not that Paul necessarily disagrees with the ancient assessment of the genesis and operation of each gift. Rather, he has a different way to assess their worth, one that has to do with a gift's contribution to the community. Because tongues cannot be understood by other people, it is not beneficial to others. In contrast, prophecy contributes to the common good because it can be understood and thus build up the entire congregation (e.g., 1 Cor. 14:2–5).

There is irony in Paul's assessment. What he sees as the greater gift of prophecy is viewed as the lesser gift in society.[8] Paul is calling the Corinthians to sacrifice their social status, the foundation of their earthly identity, to seek that which would help others more. He calls them to consider others as better than themselves by foregoing what would increase their status.

Paul redefines the issue. There is a better gift, but not in the way the Corinthians think. If the point is that the members of the body are to care for one another, their evaluation of how they are to operate depends upon what builds up the community. If the Corinthians want the greater gift, they must be willing to sacrifice their concerns about individual status. The greater gift in the body of Christ is the lesser one to the world. The kingdom infuses new meaning into what is valuable and honorable.

Paul is calling them to sacrifice, to give up what would make them important in their own society. He wants them to do an about-face from what their non-Christian neighbors and friends would think about them, to trust that what God says is better is truly better—to consider others and not just themselves, even at great personal cost (Phil. 2:3). And this is what the body of Christ is all about. It is one thing to want to help someone else. It is another thing when you make a personal sacrifice to do so, especially when that sacrifice hits close to the things you dearly value, those things that give many of us our identity.

On December 11, 1995, the Malden Mills textile plant in Lawrence, Massachusetts, burned to the ground. The company produced Polartec synthetic fleece and employed 3,000 people. Two weeks before Christmas, all of those people lost their jobs. The owner was a seventy-year-old man named Aaron Feuerstein. If he had done what many others in the textile industry expected him to do, he would have taken the insurance payout and retired. Or maybe he would have used this opportunity to move the plant to a cheaper labor market to make it more profitable. But Feuerstein lived differently. For him, the business was not about maximizing profits or being an industry leader but about being responsible for his employees. Closing down the business would have been disastrous for the employees and the town since the plant was one of the biggest employers in the area.

His Jewish faith led him in only one direction—to care for his employees. He rebuilt the plant, paid his employees while the new plant was being constructed, and covered their health insurance. He even gave every worker a Christmas bonus.[9]

What Feuerstein did was so noteworthy and unexpected he was considered a national hero and was invited to sit with President Bill Clinton at a State of the Union address. But Feuerstein did not consider his actions all that unusual. He thought it was simply natural to be concerned about his employees and the community.[10] As he told one interviewer, "It would have been unconscionable to put 3,000 people on the streets and deliver a death blow to the cities of Lawrence and Methuen."

Feuerstein refused to be shaped by the values of the culture, though he also recognized the conflict. Further along in the interview, he declared, "Maybe on paper our company is worthless to Wall Street, but I can tell you it's worth more."[11] Feuerstein understood something many of us forget: how he treated others as individuals and the impact of his business on the community mattered just as much, if not more, than the bottom line.

He also understood that committing to this meant he might have to sacrifice. The company flourished for a few years after this but then ran into severe problems. Malden Mills declared bankruptcy twice, Feuerstein was replaced as CEO, and the company was eventually sold. Many attributed the company's woes to his generosity after the fire, including his decision to rebuild the company at a cost of 130 million dollars more than what he received from the insurance company. In addition to building a state-of-the-art facility, he wanted to make it more pleasant and healthy for the workers, but the decision also helped saddle the company with a burdensome debt from which it could not recover.[12]

When interviewed about this, Feuerstein said he had no regrets about not taking the 300 million dollar insurance payout to retire to a life of luxury.[13] He considered it the right thing to do, and he said he would do the same thing again.[14] He made the decisions because he did not see himself in isolation from his employees—he was connected with them. He felt responsible for them, and because of that, the personal sacrifice was worth it. He was able to care for his workers, even if not to the extent he had hoped.

For Paul Christianity clashes with the values of the larger world in innumerable ways, but his own faith is grounded in several key foundational beliefs. Humility, rather than personal gain, enables the greater good of building the community. What contributes to the whole and to others takes precedence over individual gain. The identity of individuals as members of the family of God takes priority over social status. The unity shared with every member, their intimate connection to one another, should drive the way they treat one another. Because they belong to one another, they should seek the good of others and the good of the larger body.

We learn from the apostle that the unity of the body is not a vague or Pollyannaish concept, nor is it always compatible with the world's understanding of what unity looks like. For Paul, the nature of the body of Christ determines what is "good" for the whole (1 Cor. 12:7). So, for example, if the point of the gifts is their usefulness for the whole, it is important that they be implemented in an orderly fashion. Paul says the prophets should be able to wait their turn before speaking. Perhaps only two or three, not everyone with a prophecy, will have the chance to speak (1 Cor. 14:29). As for the tongues speakers, even though their spiritual manifestation is valid, it is not appropriate in the congregation. Not only does it not benefit the body, but it can actually hurt their witness to the outside world. For example, an unbeliever who comes to a meeting where people are speaking in an unintelligible language may simply conclude they are crazy (1 Cor. 14:23). This is why prophecy is preferred to speaking in tongues in the public gatherings. Gifts are not simply for the benefit of the individual, but also for the community.

As Paul turns the Corinthians' conceptions about what is meaningful inside out, he gives them the means not only to settle their disputes but also to truly work toward building the community. There may be disputes between groups, but this is not a battle for supremacy between different sides. Instead, they should be working together for the good of the whole, being mindful of their ultimate identity in their Savior, because the members of the body are responsible for each other. To build the body they must be willing to change their conceptions about what is good and most valuable, to not be held captive to their personal concerns, and to allow the Spirit to transform the way they consider themselves in relation to their brothers and sisters in Christ. In this way, they could have *shalom*, and in this same way, so can we.

CHAPTER 11

WHEN EVERYONE IS WRONG

Some might argue that focusing on building relationships or on learning empathy and understanding can lead to a watering down of the gospel, a softening of the hard teachings of Jesus. That is a legitimate concern and an important warning. We can be so concerned about offending someone or hurting their feelings that we don't get around to telling them important truths.

But we can also note that for Paul, this is not an either-or. Rather, as the gospel is based upon the sacrifice of Christ, the example of Christ is the foundation for the community of his followers (e.g., Phil. 2:1–11). Paul's letters say a great deal about relationships in a community where believers wrestle with conflicts over race, status, and gender. Again, there is nothing new under the sun. Yet his timeless understanding of the gospel cuts to the core of what is most important. When the believers have disputes, including racial disagreements, Paul presents the relational component as critical, even as he addresses quarrels over which side is "right."[1]

⇥⇥↗⇥⇥

Returning to Romans 14–15, we see Paul confronting a situation that likely has ethnic overtones. The Roman congregation has a problem between some who think they should eat only vegetables, not meat, and others who embrace greater freedom in their culinary indulgence. An additional area of contention concerns the sacred nature of certain days. This conflict is taking place between some Jewish believers, who still have a difficult time letting go of the requirements of the law, and some gentile believers, who have no such scruples.[2]

The situation is tense enough to catch the apostle's attention. Who is right? Do believers have this freedom in Christ, or are the Jewish believers right to honor their conscience in this way? Paul gives a straightforward answer. All foods are now clean, which means the Jewish believers' concerns about the law are unnecessary (Rom. 14:14). As a matter of doctrine, the omnivores/non-special-day observers are correct.[3] But a declaration of doctrinal correctness is more of an afterthought than Paul's main point. Instead, he is worried about the relationships between the believers. He is upset with the way they are treating one another, and he holds both parties accountable.

He says, "Let not the one who eats despise the one who abstains, and let not the one who abstains pass judgment on the one who eats, for God has welcomed him"

(14:3 ESV). This is an amazing statement. Paul acknowledges that one side is objectively right in their theological evaluation of the immediate situation—there is no need to eat only vegetables. However, he faults *both* for the way they are treating one another. The theologically correct are as much at fault for these problems in the community as the theologically incorrect. In short, rightness and wrongness for the theological problem of food is separate from—and perhaps of lesser concern in this particular situation—than the relational problems they are dealing with. Paul recognizes there is another layer to the situation. There is also the problem of how the Roman believers deal with the issue among themselves, and Paul sees that how they are treating each other is destroying the unity of the body of Christ.

Paul's instructions to the Romans deal with both parties in the dispute. He resolves the overt theological issue rather quickly. He tells the ones who believe they can eat everything not to pass judgment on those whose faith is "weak" (Rom. 14:1–2). He then informs the vegetable-only eaters that those they disagree with are also accepted by God, so they are not to condemn them (Rom. 14:3–4).[4]

More important, and extensive, is Paul's discussion of their relational failure. He unpacks the nature of their quarreling. While Paul elsewhere talks about the dangers of division (for example, in 1 Corinthians 1:10 and Philippians 4:2), this discussion is especially fascinating in the way he identifies specific attitudes on each side of the dispute. He does not merely give a general command to love and tolerate one another. Each side has wronged the other in a unique way (Rom. 14:3–4, 10). The side that celebrated their freedom in Christ has succumbed to the temptation to "despise" (ESV) or be contemptuous of those who adamantly maintained their traditions. Believing they are the enlightened ones, they look down on those backward people still clinging to their old ways. But the more conservative party has their own problems. They are guilty of condemning those ignorant people who carelessly and callously disregard the sacred traditions and abandon cherished ways. One group assumes a position of moral superiority, while the other takes pride in pointing out someone else's perceived fatal error.

Paul challenges both their failure to live out the command to love one another and the way they see themselves in respect to one another. Paul has just told them all of God's commandments are summed up in one phrase: "Love your neighbor as yourself" (Rom. 13:9; cf. Lev. 19:18). The Romans should know that "love does no harm to a neighbor" (Rom. 13:10). They are not to consider themselves "more highly" than they should (Rom. 12:3), yet they are positioning themselves as better than others, just in different ways.

Regardless of who is "right" or "wrong," they both have the wrong attitude. In fact, we can identify two distinct problems. First, whether one is "right" on the issue does not absolve one's responsibility for properly regarding those on the opposite side of the issue. In other words, a person can have a correct evaluation of an issue (here it would be the omnivores) yet subsequently sin in the relationship with the other person. In Rome, each party in the dispute faces a particular temptation to sin against the other. Perhaps we face the same temptations, whichever "side" we are on.

The same attitudes found among the Roman believers can catch any of us at any time on any issue. No one has a monopoly on contempt or condemnation. These attitudes can appear suddenly or gradually—and without our noticing they have taken residence in our souls. We can be particularly blind to them when we are absolutely certain we are right.

Many years ago, I was taking classes at a very conservative school in the South, one that said women should not wear pants, had separate stairways for men and women, and did not believe the more sensational gifts of the Spirit in 1 Corinthians 12 continued today. Not having the same scruples over dress and staircases, as well as having spent much time in charismatic circles, I found myself feeling a bit superior to the people there because they did not seem to have the same freedom in Christ I did. Yet by the end of my time there, while my beliefs on those matters remained unchanged, I found that my attitudes had changed significantly. I experienced a deep conviction about how I had initially regarded my brothers and sisters in Christ, as well as a sense of the lack of the Spirit in my own life.

By the time I left, I had a new respect for my floormate's observation about how refreshing it was that the undergraduate men and women always dressed so neatly because of the dress code. Everyone wore clean, fresh clothing, and I gained an appreciation for the prevailing modesty on campus. It all contributed to a comfortable and relaxed demeanor.

I was convicted about my condescension toward their view of the Spirit on the day a missionary spoke in chapel. He spoke with passion about his desire for God to save the lost, his voice cracking as he was momentarily overcome with emotion. It was evident the Spirit was moving in him for something I tended to neglect, nothing less than Jesus's Great Commission (Matt. 28:19). At that moment I realized how foolish I was to believe that only people who believed exactly what I believed could participate in the powerful moving of the Spirit. I saw how arrogant I was to think I was superior for my more self-centered view of the Spirit. My perspective on the school changed as a result. Even more, I realized that in my heart I had despised the people at this school for not being as "enlightened" as I was. Whether or not I was correct in my assessment of their views, I had fallen far short in treating them as brothers and sisters in Christ.

I have found myself on the other side of this as well. I spent over fifteen years on what our school calls the "Doctrinal Review Team," comprised of numerous theologically trained faculty who interview potential new hires. We scrutinize their responses to our doctrinal statement and make an evaluation as to whether they might be a good fit for our school. Although I am not sure how good a job I actually did, all these years working on this team nevertheless have made me highly attuned to look for deviations from our doctrinal statement. I find this sensitivity carries over into unconscious evaluations of other Christian organizations who do not have the same convictions we do. This can include what are generally called the "grey areas," or instances where Scripture is not clear on how believers should act. I find my evaluations can easily slip into personal judgment. I find myself labelling them as those who are straying from the faith or do not truly understand the gospel, while I am theologically astute and faithful. Regardless of the accuracy of my assessment, I am confident my pride in my own judgment of someone else's fallenness or unacceptability is not pleasing to Christ.

I think it is a natural human desire to want to protect our sense of self, often by imagining ourselves to be better than others. But Scripture calls us to edify the other person, not bring them down in order to build ourselves up. Paul reminds us that we must be willing to look unflinchingly at what may be wrong in our own hearts, even when we are convinced we are right. Being right on one thing does not mean we are right on everything. I may hold the truth and still sin against someone else. I can be right and wrong at the same time, and there is always the need for humility and grace.

One of the most remarkable aspects of Paul's letters is the way he can pronounce one side of a dispute as "correct" yet speak to both sides in terms of how they are relating to each other. In doing so, he reminds us that we must seek to discern precisely what is at stake in each situation, which cannot always be reduced to a single issue. A preoccupation with doctrine can cause us to neglect the command to love one another, while our desire to maintain relationship could lead to overlooking error. We are called both to evaluate wisely and to search our hearts for when we have not properly regarded our brother or sister in Christ, a fellow believer "for whom Christ died" (1 Cor. 8:11).

$$\overline{\diagup\vert\diagdown}$$

As much as I felt marginalized and rejected growing up, I made another discovery as well: some of my classmates were worse off than I was. I had a little group of friends and a certain place in the school's social eco-system. But others spent their days in isolation and didn't have a warm group of companions. They stood out in their aloneness, and I am ashamed to say I was among those who made fun of and marginalized them. The reason was that selfishly it made me feel better. It offered the relief of making someone else the target instead of me.

It's difficult to overcome the hardness of the human heart. It's easy to deceive ourselves into thinking we are the only ones who are right. And we will always be hobbled by personal limitations. I doubt there is a perfect way in this world to achieve racial harmony, one that is free of any tension, awkwardness, offense, or hurt. There is no perfect solution because we are imperfect people. Rather, there is One who is perfect and *is* the solution. Perhaps we can clumsily learn to grow together as his body in grace and humility as we seek to become more like Christ to one another, even as he slowly and pains-takingly transforms us.

In the real world, our desires, intentions, and perspectives often clash as we meet people with different backgrounds, life experiences, and wounds that are unknown to us. When difficult or awkward situations come up, it is all too easy to focus on what we see as the unreasonableness of the other person's position. I may think, for example, that someone is too easily hurt and not accepting responsibility for themselves. Perhaps that person may see me as insensitive and unwilling to acknowledge that I have done something to hurt them. The situation becomes immeasurably more complex when both of us have a point.

When Paul tells us to care for one another, he does not mean to pretend everything is fine even if it's not or ignore when someone is hurt or an injustice or violation occurs. Paul is realistic about the challenges believers faced in creating a community that crossed racial, gender, and status boundaries, boundaries that were just as, if not more, rigid and fraught with potential for conflict than we have today. But he also knew he was up against a universal human problem, that race was one of many avenues through which people could murder one another in their hearts (1 John 3:15; Matt. 5:21–22), and only Christ was the solution.

It was no easy task for the early Christian community to overcome longstanding hostilities, prejudices, and misconceptions about each other. The Roman Christians' conflict was ultimately not about vegetables but about themselves and how they loved or failed to love each other. Paul wanted them to know that in Christ and through the Spirit they could become an intimate and unified community. Their corporate identity as brothers and sisters in Christ could foster their unity. This provided the lens to understand the significance of their racial differences. It neither ignored those differences nor made them primary. Instead, it gave them a way to live together. Tensions would naturally arise from their differences. But the believers would learn not just to live together but, even more, to love one another as Christ had loved them. Their corporate sense of belonging to one another and to Christ would be the means of producing a peace that ultimately could come only from the Spirit.[5]

PART 3

BELONGING TO GOD

You belong to Christ, and
Christ belongs to God.

—1 CORINTHIANS 3:23 NASB

CHAPTER 12

KNOWING OUR PLACE

Maybe you've heard the saying, "Perspective is everything." While I'm not sure it's that all-encompassing, our perspective certainly seems to make a difference in how we understand the world and our place in it. It's not hard to find examples of this. I recently heard the story of JFK and the janitor. President Kennedy was visiting NASA during the heyday of the US-Soviet space race when he met a janitor. JFK asked the man what he did at the agency. The man responded, "I'm helping put a man on the moon!" That story is reminiscent of an older story about Christopher Wren, the English architect who designed St. Paul's Cathedral. When he asked the men working there what they were doing, the first one replied, "I am cutting a piece of stone." The second one said, "I am earning five shillings twopence a day." And the third proudly answered, "I am helping Sir Christopher Wren build a beautiful cathedral."[1]

Perspective guides how we think about what we do

and how we think about other people. When I think about my job as a paycheck, my students are simply a means to that end. The result is that I will fulfill the requirements to get that check but nothing more, or at least nothing above and beyond what others might notice or that I can put in my year-end report. When I am focused on myself, I neglect to see the person checking out my groceries, talking to me from the call center, or delivering my mail as real people instead of someone who exists solely to take care of my needs.

How we see the larger picture impacts the way we view and treat others. When I was growing up, I thought I was different from the rest of the world, and that crushed me. When I went to college, I learned there were others like me, and that realization was freeing. When I began to see things from my White husband's perspective and not just my own, I was challenged further and grew.

On the one hand, God hates injustice, and we are called to peace as members of one body. On the other hand, it is easy to overestimate our role in bringing about gospel goals, and we should be extremely wary of the trap of being self-congratulatory for what we accomplish. Humility and dependence on God were the hallmarks of people like Paul, who constantly pointed out that in whatever he did, he was only an instrument, and God was the true Maker and Creator (1 Cor. 3:7).

Paul knew the dangers of putting "confidence in the flesh" (Phil. 3:4), the seductive self-righteousness that comes from having the "right" beliefs, following the "right" rules, or being a member of the "right" group

(Phil. 3:5–6). His imagined righteousness led him to persecute the followers of the man he would later follow as his Lord and Savior, the one for whose sake he would consider all his worldly accomplishments and pedigree as garbage and loss (Phil. 3:7–8). What Paul describes is our uncanny ability to take our good intentions and use them to serve our own interests and placate our insecurities, especially when we place confidence in our ability to make things right. But our efforts may look quite different when we pursue first the *one* who actually can make all things right. This is the path Paul chooses. He would trade in his own zeal and righteousness to gain the person and righteousness of Christ. He would learn who he truly was in relation to the God he served. As much as this can sound like clichéd Christian-speak, he and the other New Testament writers would show us the need to live most fundamentally from the truth that God is God and we are not.

⚛

Revelation 7:9 provides an amazing view of heaven. We see a great gathering of people "from every nation, tribe, people and language" around the throne of God. The people are too numerous to be counted. They are from all areas of the earth. They stand in perfect unity, gathered together before God with no animosity or hatred, enraptured in worship of God and Jesus. This description of God's people indicates that this multiethnic diversity is a significant aspect of the kingdom of God and that it is good. God has extended his offer of salvation to all, creating a community drawn from all corners of the earth and including all nations and peoples. The gathering in Revelation is a picture of what God desires.[2]

Because of this, the passage is rightly used to justify an understanding that the church is a multicultural church. However, I can't help but wonder if there is something else going on as well. Yes, this picture shows us that unity and diversity are important to God, but this perspective still seems to be missing something critical. The scene shows us a *result*, the gathering of a diverse people around God's throne. But what *caused* this amazing assembly in the first place? Why are these diverse peoples now able to be together without the acrimony and warring that thwart our best intentions?

I have listened to talks on reconciliation which give the impression that if we simply acknowledge things like, "Unity in diversity is good," or we create enough diversity in our particular situation, then miraculously all of our previous difficulties should suddenly go "poof" and disappear. Knowing where we want to go is good, but it doesn't mean we've arrived. As we know, racial and relational conflict has been with us for a long time. We appear to be quite good at it. While we say we want peace and reconciliation, too often we exemplify what James says when he writes: "What causes fights and quarrels among you? Don't they come from your desires that battle within you? You desire but do not have, so you kill. You covet but cannot get what you want, so you quarrel and fight" (James 4:1–2).

Our present situation accords quite well with what

we've seen throughout biblical history. Human beings prefer fighting with one another over getting along, not to mention loving one another. The other person does not give us what we think we deserve, so we get angry. They are not who we think they should be, so we judge. We point the finger at someone else's sin, but we fail to see our own.

Our continued conflicts reveal that our nice sayings and positive thoughts are like putting paint over rust. There is something deeper, and we can't just cover it up. I hear much said today about the importance of being united in our diversity. But we also have to talk about the many reasons why we have been divided for so long. It's likely more complicated than just a lack of knowledge, will, or desire. It may be that we need to take a long look at ourselves and what else we are doing or not doing to make things so difficult. If not, we run the very real risk of simply spinning our wheels, or maybe even making things worse.

How can we get from the mess we have here on earth to that blissful, idyllic scene in heaven? Should we start by trying to get all these different groups together? Does one group bear more responsibility than the others? Is there a special method of communication or conflict-resolution technique that those saints learned that brought them together? As helpful as answers to these questions might be, I believe the scene itself contains an important clue about where that unity all begins, something that makes our efforts rather perilous if we miss it.

That clue is the *throne* of God.

Being in the presence of and standing or kneeling before God's throne directly impacts us. Before that throne, we must acknowledge God's bigness and our smallness, his holiness and our unworthiness. Before the throne there is no pretense of our own righteousness or illusion of our supremacy over others. God's throne humbles us. It breaks down our defenses and shows us the futility of self-dependence. God's throne is the great equalizer for sinners.

Crucially, God's multicultural people in Revelation are gathered in worship *before the throne*. Their hearts are oriented to their Creator, fully aware of their complete inadequacy and his all-surpassing adequacy. Being before the throne may be the position—the only position—that allows us to overcome all the pettiness and meanness that causes our division and pain.

The *modus operandi* these days often seems to go like this: we begin with a claim to moral superiority for whichever side we are on, and then we heap scathing judgment on the ignorant and/or evil transgressors on the other side who are not as enlightened, smart, or virtuous as we are. In other words, I want to be on the "right" side because it makes me feel good about myself, even if I have to disparage someone else.

When I read my Bible, though, I see a lot of warnings against this. Warnings against having a high opinion of myself; warnings against the danger of relying on our righteousness. We are "accountable to God" (Rom. 3:19) if we do this, which we should all find rather frightening, given Scripture's assessment of who we really are:

There is no one righteous, not even one;

There is no one who understands;

There is no one who seeks God.

All have turned away,

they have together become worthless;

there is no one who does good,

not even one. (Rom. 3:10–12)

Paul also warns us that we bear responsibility for how we consider ourselves and others. He says rather ominously: "At whatever point you judge another, you are condemning yourself, because you who pass judgment do the same things. . . . So when you, a mere human being, pass judgment on them and yet do the same things, do you think you will escape God's judgment?" (Rom. 2:1, 3).

If all this is true, then we should make sure we keep who we are, who God is, and why that matters in the forefront of our minds.[3] Thinking more of ourselves than we should is a recipe for disaster. Proverbs 1:7 reminds us of the importance of perspective, since the "fear of the LORD is beginning of knowledge." Without the right posture, we are "fools" who "despise wisdom," which is hardly the solution for solving the world's problems. Scripture reminds us over and over again that we should begin by knowing that we are not God and we serve and worship the one who really *is* God.

Y ears ago, I had a conversation with a wise colleague about a current social issue and those involved in it, thoughts I was personally rather pleased with. My colleague responded, "But what do they *do*?" Without going into the specifics of the exchange or the topic, suffice it to say I was duly reminded of the need to consider how thoughts and ideas should lead to practical action, which is more challenging for someone like me, who always comes out as a "thinker" (or "dreamer") rather than a "doer" on every personality test I've ever taken.

But while talking about our personal posture may not be as concrete as, say, "Join a protest," or "Run for office," I do believe it has significant practical implications. When we are acutely, painfully aware of the state of our hearts, it changes what we do and how we do it. The saints before the throne are in awe of God. In their worship, they know their true place and who they truly are. And that is of supreme importance.

When I consider this need for awe, my mind goes to Isaiah 6, where Isaiah encounters God in heaven. I first recall learning about Isaiah 6 as a young Christian reading the story of Jim Elliot, the missionary who was one of five people killed in an attempt to evangelize the Waodani people in Ecuador in the 1950s.[4] For those who are not familiar with Elliot, he became a Christian hero as a result of his martyrdom. He was young, handsome, smart, and articulate. He had seemingly endless potential. But Elliot and his companions confounded the world by trying to reach a tribe known to be extremely violent and dangerous to outsiders. After their tragic deaths, even the world noticed what they had done, as *Life* maga-zine dedicated ten pages to their mission. People were captivated by the thought of these young men with such promise sacrificing their lives for something they knew could likely, and eventually did, end in their deaths.

For Elliot, Jesus's commands were reason enough to undertake the perilous mission, as his widow, Elisabeth, wrote in her book, *Through Gates of Splendor*. One portion of Scripture that inspired Elliot was this passage in Isaiah. He wrote in his diary, "What else is worthwhile in this life? I have heard of nothing better. 'Lord, send me!'"[5]

Looking up the passage as a young Christian, I learned that Elliot was quoting Isaiah 6:8, where Isaiah stands before the throne of God. Isaiah is overwhelmed by the presence of the infinite, holy God on his throne in heaven. When God asks him, "Whom shall I send? And who will go for us?" Isaiah's response is simple, straightforward, and unflinching: "Here am I. Send me!" I found those words inspiring. Elliot, like Isaiah, would go wherever God sent him, to do whatever God wanted. He was willing. He was available. He was ready. Isaiah 6:8 quickly became one of my favorite verses.

As time went on, though, I pondered another aspect of Isaiah's words that I had missed. It was why and how he was able to make that bold proclamation, for it was being in the presence of God that made Isaiah say those words. All Isaiah can do is lament his unworthiness and uncleanness that stand out so powerfully next to the holi-ness of God (Is. 6:5). In the presence of the great and holy God, he can do nothing except realize his wretchedness.

He no longer has any pretense about his goodness or ability. He is broken and humbled, helpless and hopeless in himself.

Now he is able to be sent, or perhaps better, he is in a place where God can make him into someone able to be sent.

Isaiah's willingness to go was the result of standing before the throne of the God of the universe. He shows us that we begin not with our noble intentions, or magnificent skills and knowledge, but rather the opposite—the profound and utterly devastating realization of our inability and our deceptive and sinful motives.[6] God doesn't want Isaiah to run out like a gunslinger or superhero, fired up to take on the bad guys and make everything right in the world. God needs Isaiah to have a realistic view of himself so Isaiah can actually be useful. In the presence of God, illusions of our competency and merit-earning goodness are shattered. Before the greatness of God, all we can do is fall down in despair at our total inability and our treacherous hearts. But the loss of our hopes for personal significance and confidence in our individual competence makes it possible to submit ourselves to God and walk in the Spirit Jesus promised us (Gal. 5:16; John 14:15–17).

This is the posture of the saints in Revelation 7. They are united in the presence of the awe-inspiring, all-humbling God, as we will be. Before the Almighty God, all sense of personal superiority will melt away. We will see God for who he is, and as a result we will see ourselves for who we are. Only the overwhelming nature of

God will be able to overcome our insatiable human thirst for significance and power, a thirst that drives us to seek advantage over the other, too often at the expense of the other. Only complete submission to our Creator can cause us to truly come together, as natural human barriers fade into insignificance through our collective realization of utter dependence on the Creator. Differences will remain, but our compulsion to ignore, leverage, or abuse those for our own gain will not. We will see others as those whom we are with and for rather than against. All this happens when we stand in awe of God.

CHAPTER 13

IN AWE

Awe matters. You don't have to believe in Jesus to understand the impact of being in the presence of something greater than yourself. Some psychologists have done a fascinating study on what happens when we are in awe, which they define as "that often-positive feeling of being in the presence of something vast that transcends our understanding of the world."[1] It implies seeing something bigger than ourselves that stretches our knowledge of the world and gives us perspective on who we are in that world. In short, awe creates a type of humility, which then influences our relationships with one another.

The psychologists concluded that experiencing awe can be helpful for building caring community. For one, it aids in the challenging task of taking us out of ourselves so we can then be concerned about others (which would seem rather helpful if we're talking about something like reconciliation). This means that as much as I might want to be the center of the universe, there are actually very important reasons for not making myself the center of the universe.

Naturally, to test their theory, the psychologists conducted some experiments.[2] In one they asked people how much they experienced awe in their lives, as in seeing wonder and beauty in the world. They then gave those people ten lottery tickets that they could either keep or share with other participants who did not receive the tickets. Those who reported experiencing more awe in their lives were more likely to be generous with the tickets than those with less awe.

A second experiment involved taking people to a grove of very tall trees, over 200 feet tall. There they instructed one group to look up at the trees for a minute. They instructed the others to look at a nearby building. Then, as things tend to go in these experiments, a staged "event" occurred. Someone stumbled and dropped a bunch of pens. The researchers noted that those who had been looking up at the trees helped pick up more pens than those who had looked at the building.

While I know there are limits to what hard and fast conclusions we can draw from things like picking up pens and lottery-ticket giveaways, I still find the idea of how we respond to awe fascinating. Awe, the psychologists concluded, helps people think of themselves more humbly, as a smaller part of something larger. As a result, we become less narcissistic and more attuned to others. I can see this in my own life. The bigger and more powerful I feel, the greater my temptation to look down on others. The more I see my smallness after experiencing awe, the more I view others with compassion.

If just looking at trees for one minute can make us more caring and other-focused, imagine what happens when we are in the presence of the one who created not only the trees but everything that exists. Significantly, the first scene of worship of God on the throne in Revelation is based on God being the Creator of all things. (4:11). This part of the foundation of our worship comes from giving honor and glory to the one who made us.

Awe helps me know I am not the center of the universe. Awe of the one who is the center of the universe makes me realize this even more. When we are in awe of God and his majesty, we are transformed, and the result is something like what Isaiah and the nations experienced around the throne of God.

But as much as I am aware of the importance of awe, too much of my life is spent without it.

In Romans 1, Paul presents a rather bleak picture of what happens without a proper awe of God. He argues that from the very beginning, we didn't worship and serve God like we were created to do. In fact, not only did we not do that, but we did something foolish. Although we were created by a glorious, immortal, and eternally powerful God, we gave our awe not to the one who made us but to created things. Think about that for a second. The created things worshiped themselves. They cut themselves off from the source of their being to try to make themselves the source of life and meaning.

I'm not sure how that hits you, but it strikes me as being completely backward, not to mention doomed to failure.

Paul doesn't pull any punches in telling us the results of our misplaced awe, when we didn't worship God as we were created to do.

> For since the creation of the world God's invisible qualities—his eternal power and divine nature—have been clearly seen, being understood from what has been made, so that people are without excuse. For although they knew God, they neither glorified him as God nor gave thanks to him, but their thinking became futile and their foolish hearts were darkened. (Rom. 1:20–21)

In choosing to reject their Creator, in choosing the wrong perspective and heart posture, people fell into a tragic spiral. As they served "created things rather than the Creator," their thoughts become futile and their hearts hardened. They were given over to and consumed by "the sinful desires of their hearts" (Rom. 1:24–25). In essence, they got what they wanted. They got to go their own way. They got to follow their own desires, which, without God, lead inexorably to conflict and destruction. Not only does James tell us that our desires are the source of our problems with each other (James 4:1), but Paul also reveals to us that the end product of being turned over to ourselves is "wickedness, evil, greed and depravity . . . envy, murder, strife, deceit and malice" (Rom. 1:29).

We may think at least we personally don't exhibit all those characteristics on that list, but Paul is clear that we all do the same or similar things (Rom. 2:1). More importantly, Paul is simply describing what happens when God lets us go our own way. When we don't focus on worshiping God as we were created to do, when we prefer to worship ourselves, we pay the price in our own souls and together.

I was at a grocery store, hurrying about as I was huffing and puffing about how long it was taking, because I had many *very important* things to do. I had my groceries unloaded and ready to pay and I glanced back to notice a petite older woman behind me. Annoyance swiftly gave way to the realization of her . . .

If I can harbor such thoughts on a simple trip to the grocery store, what might occur in more serious situations? When I think about something that has happened to me (a slight, a slur, an insult, an injustice), my heart can react differently. Sometimes a slight impacts me very little. Other times, when I am feeling particularly gracious (at least in theory), I may pray for that person. too often, I nurture the grievance, mulling it ov over, sometimes leading to outrage, other tim When that happens, I am always amaze those thoughts can penetrate and distort n I end up with beliefs about the person the infraction that I am later shocke

And I am also shocked wh can happen in any spher "side" I happen to be gender sinned against turning into the sinners. But reflexively protecting doctrine can lead to pride in my insightfulness, a congratulatory self-righteousness for my astute observations, and a calloused heart that uses judgments against those I see as less doctrinally sound to justify doing nothing about a very real problem. In either scenario, my deceitful heart may cause me to pat myself on the back for my noble motives and incisive insights when in my heart I am doing the murdering Jesus warned against (Matt. 5:21–22). There is a huge difference between acknowledging that all people are created in the image of God—in other words, like knowing a correct answer that I can put down on an exam—and treating people like I actually believe it.

When I see sin or am sinned against, reactions such as hardness, condemnation, bitterness, or a desire for retribution may be understandable, but that doesn't make them right. It is hard to imagine a unified church built on such reactions. And most certainly they do not fall within the range of "whatever is true, whatever is noble, whatever is right, whatever is pure, whatever is lovely, whatever is admirable" that I am supposed to think about (Phil. 4:8).

Nature abhors a vacuum, so if my heart is not directed toward the awe of God, I will worship something else—myself, a cause, an idea. In commitment to my self-appointed idol, whatever it is, I can forget to see people as those who have great worth because they have been created in the image of God. I cease to treat them as people.

We were created to honor and praise our Creator. We need to worship because without that focus on something bigger than ourselves, the Author of everything, we cannot help but descend into self-centeredness, with predictable, tragic results. A quick look at what is happening today, around the world, should be all we need to tell us what we are letting ourselves become.

※

While I think most people would agree that unity is important and desirable, I think we would also agree that true unity is really, really difficult.

My husband and I recently watched the classic movie *Gandhi* for the zillionth time. I usually find it inspiring. This time I found it depressing.

This time I paid more attention to how the two religious groups, the Muslims and Hindus, banded together to gain rule over their own country. Bitter enemies, they were able to put aside their hatred of each other to unify against the British. Then after their mission was completed, the country erupted into sectarian violence, and the groups started attacking and killing each other. Their fragile peace, one that accomplished something incredible, disintegrated as soon as the common goal was accomplished.[3]

Conflict is the never-ending story of human history. We hurt each other because we are sinful. And since we are all sinful (Rom. 3:23), we should assume that unity is extraordinarily difficult. It is particularly difficult because we are so different.

A cheap type of unity is built on sameness. It is cheap because it is easy. Getting along with people who are like me takes a lot less effort. Sameness is comforting. Here are people who sound like me, who will not challenge me, who will affirm me. Of course, there can be some very good things about that. I enjoy sharing ideas or hobbies with those who have similar interests so I can be inspired and supported by people who understand me. Coming together for a common cause can accomplish great things. It can be easier to go deeper in a relationship if you already have a shared understanding with someone else.

The problem is that sameness demands little of me. It seems geared toward validating and building up who I am (by the presence of other people just like me!). It does not challenge me to give up my desire to be the center of everything, where I can stay cozy and comfortable in the belief that all good revolves around what ultimately benefits me or that my perspective is the only one that really matters. Unity built on sameness has a hard time lasting when difficulties arise. In these moments, unavoidable differences come to light, and the superficial veneer of togetherness gives way to our uglier selves.

The challenge of real unity makes the gathering before the throne a remarkable sight. God does not dissolve differences, such as returning everyone to one language or creating a single nation. Rather, these differences of nations, tribes, peoples, and languages are transcended in worship of the one God, even while they remain.[4]

What does this unity look like, and how is it accomplished? In Ephesians the mystery of God was the unity of two groups, Jew and gentile into "one new man," where those who historically hated one another would be willing to die for one another. This required a love that demands humility, that requires sacrifice. This is how it could last eternally. And we should not overlook how in this letter, as Paul talks about a unity that would transcend generations of hatred, he begins by pointing both groups to the greatness of God and the greatness of their salvation.

> Praise be to the God and Father of our Lord Jesus Christ, who has blessed us in the heavenly realms with every spiritual blessing in Christ. For he chose us in him before the creation of the world to be holy and blameless in his sight. In love he predestined us for adoption to sonship through Jesus Christ, in accordance with his pleasure and will—to the praise of his glorious grace, which he has freely given us in the One he loves. In him we have redemption through his blood, the forgiveness of sins, in accordance with the riches of God's grace that he lavished on us. With all wisdom and understanding, he made known to us the mystery of his will according to his good pleasure, which he purposed in Christ, to be put into effect when the times reach their fulfillment—to bring unity to all things in heaven and on earth under Christ. (Eph. 1:3–10)

Paul makes clear that the blessings that Jew and gentile share are from the same great God, who created the world and made us his children, who has given us the riches of his grace and in the end will bring all things together in unity. He does not focus on one group over the other. His point is that they must begin by honoring and praising God for his blessings of salvation to everyone. Within this overarching context Paul can go on to talk about their oneness as Jew and gentile.[5]

In all the talk these days about the importance of having diversity, I can't help but wonder what that really means. I hear that it is important to get different perspectives, to hear different stories, to have representation from different types of people. It's hard to disagree with that. There can be a lot of good in diversity. I have seen it in my own life.

But this seems to miss a more foundational starting point. With all the conversation about how this type of diversity is good, I honestly don't see Scripture telling us that our main goal is to *pursue* it. Diversity was a natural hallmark of the early church, reflecting a universal gospel in which salvation was available to all. Therefore, the point was not that the early Christians should focus their efforts on creating a group made up of a variety of peoples. Rather, it was about how the Spirit could create *peace* among an already diverse group who were called to live together.

Having this slight change in perspective doesn't mean that certain pursuits of diversity in the church are wrong or that such diversity isn't good. Rather, it means we begin from who we already are as the body of Christ and therefore with the nature of the relationships among all of us who belong to him. The church was a puzzle in the ancient world because the gospel brought together those who had previously been separated—Jew and gentile, slave and free, male and female. As such, it was undeniably diverse. But the amazing thing was that rather than producing the expected conflict among the different groups, or everyone being separated according to traditional means, all could worship the same God in the same place and in the same way. In this oneness, Jews and gentiles were not to hate one another, the rich were not to flaunt their wealth and privilege over the poor, and men were not to proclaim superiority over women.

The problem—and potential—for the church was how those who were previously at odds with or separated from one another could come together, how they could transcend conventional human barriers and antagonisms to become truly one, the body of Christ and the family of God. The universal gospel Jesus preached would bring together those who had been hostile to one another, but it was also the means to overcome hatred or divisions, whatever they were, in whatever state the church found itself.

My brother Leonard once remarked to me how he and Marie had such a hard time getting along when they were growing up. It was likely the result of having such divergent, clashing personalities. Their relationship changed as they grew older, but as kids it led to a lot of strife (such as the infamous incident when Len punched Marie before the photo). Families are often that way. We don't get to choose who we are related to, and often we are incredibly different from each other. But we are still a family, and we are called to live together nonetheless. At times we are successful, at other times wildly unsuccessful. But we are meant to be together.

I wonder if we've gotten some of the priorities and perspective around unity and diversity a bit muddled. So much of our focus is on pursuing diversity. Certainly there can be benefit to that. But again, perhaps we need to start with who we *are* rather than what we want to do. Scripture reminds us that the human condition *is* diversity, and this leads to some important truths. Since we are so different, unity is unbelievably difficult because of our very human inclinations to disparage, dominate, or harm those who are not like us. Becoming truly one is only possible if we overcome our human limitations. This kind of unity is only possible in the kingdom of God as members of the family of God in Christ.

The outpouring of the Spirit at Pentecost means that in this diverse unity everyone—young and old, male and female—can be proclaimers of the gospel (Acts 2:17–21). The kingdom is not limited to the most privileged and highly regarded in society. It is a new type of community.

So when Paul talks about the body of Christ, he doesn't tell them to make the local church Jew and gentile. He says that "whether" they are Jew or gentile, they are one (1 Cor. 12:13). In other words, he doesn't directly address the point of whether they should try to create diversity in their congregations. Instead, he focuses on fundamental truths about the nature of their new life in Christ: the universal nature of the gospel makes membership in the body available to all, and even when the church is made up of diverse groups that would naturally hate each another, they are to show the love of Christ to one another. In this way, the church's task is to recognize the essential nature of their new existence so they can live out what God made them to be, in whatever their situation they find themselves.

God brings together people who are so different that in the flesh it would be difficult or even impossible to get along, much less truly love one another. But somehow God chooses this humanly impossible situation to show something that is only possible in Christ. He brings together people of many nations, tribes, and tongues, and we are to love and care for one another as Christ loves us rather than harm and battle for superiority over one another.

As I look around today and see incredible progress on many fronts—scientific, economic, technological—it seems we have made little progress, if any, on how we treat one another. We are far less civil, far less kind, far less considerate. We are less able to honor and bless one another and quicker to respond in anger, offense, and blame. We are increasingly shocked at what people are willing to say and do to one another.

Perhaps we can attain some tenuous approximation of "unity" for a time through our own efforts, but the profound reconciliation and peace that we desire always eludes us—it may be even further away than ever. As we ponder how we can ever achieve this kind of peace, it may be relevant to notice something else about those scenes in Revelation, namely, that the worship is before both God *and* the Lamb.

What strikes me here is that of all the images of Jesus in Revelation, he is worshiped—*worshiped*—as the slain, sacrificed-for-us Lamb (Rev. 5 and 7).[6] Not the fearsome rider on the white horse (Rev. 19:11–16). Not the one like a magnificent son of man (1:13). Not even as the powerful Lion of the tribe of Judah (5:5).[7] All of these would seem like more natural fits for a majestic throne room scene. And yet the Lamb, still bearing the marks of slaughter, is the focus of worship (5:6).[8]

This suggests that we should connect the awe-inspiringness of Jesus with his sacrificial work, his humility. At first that may sound counterintuitive. Aren't we awed by greatness, something that causes admiration and makes us feel small? But perhaps there are two different types of greatness and awe here. One type relates to the *God-who-is-so-amazing-and-all-powerful-and-holy-that-I-feel-completely-overwhelmed-and-unworthy-in-his-presence* type of awe. The other is connected with Jesus and his humility, which leads to a *this-makes-me-see-how-selfish-and-self-centered-I-am-which-makes-me-want-to-become-a-better-person* type of awe you get when you are in the presence of pure goodness and selflessness. The first is awe of God on the throne. The second is awe of Jesus, who suffered and died for us. Both give a piercing reflection of our shortcomings and compel us to change by pulling us out of our small perspective to what matters much, much more. Both help us know our true place. Both transform us.

When I am painfully aware of my smallness and pettiness, I have to ask myself, what grounds for superiority or personal demands do I have over someone else? If I were to really know my true place, how could I not love and care about my wounded neighbor, who is equally valued by God and created in his image? Maybe this kind of worship, which makes abundantly clear that I am only the created and not the Creator (Rev. 4:11), is the only way I can escape the overwhelming gravitational pull of the desire to make myself the point of everything and grasp as much as I can for myself.[9]

What might it look like when our hearts are so rightly ordered?

A tragedy that took place on July 17, 2015, in Charleston, South Carolina, still looms large in my memory as an astounding example of what it means to have hearts that are awed by Jesus. That day Dylann Roof shot and killed nine people at Emmanuel African Methodist Episcopal Church. He admitted that he specifically wanted to kill them because they were Black.[10] He did so after being welcomed into their Bible study and apparently almost didn't go through with his plan because "they were so nice to him."[11]

In addition to his horrifying actions, what shocked many people was the reaction of the survivors and their relatives. Although they wanted justice, they also prayed for him. They refused to hate him. They *forgave* him.[12]

They rightly recognized the need for justice, for

those "governing authorities" in Romans 13 to make and enforce laws that promote the good and punish the bad. But on a personal level, they knew the cost of reacting with vengeance and bitterness. As Bethane Middleton-Brown, who lost a sister, said, "I wanted to hate you, but my faith tells me no. I wanted to remain angry and bitter, but my view of life won't let me."[13]

As I read these accounts, I couldn't help but be in awe. These families could have given in to completely understandable emotions. The world, including myself, would have sympathized with their rage. But they did not surrender to those natural impulses. They saw that there were multiple layers to this situation, and rightness in one area does not justify wrongness in another. They did not want to fall into the soul-destroying spiral listed in Romans 1.

People like this shine an unflattering light on my self-centeredness. But they also make me want to be kinder and more forgiving, to be more patient, to have a bigger heart, to be like those Paul writes about in 2 Corinthians 3:18, who "with unveiled faces contemplate the Lord's glory" and are "being transformed into his image."

Worshiping the Lamb doesn't mean we sacrifice justice. Far from it. God's throne shows that he is still righteous and demands righteousness. That doesn't change. But the presence of the Lamb shows us there is something else as well. We are awed as we realize that Jesus's way of selflessness is so far from what we are actually doing and yet know deep down is the way we need to be.

I need to be transformed by both kinds of awe, an awe that causes me to know that someone is far greater than myself, and an awe that makes me want to be a better kind of self. I want the two kinds of awe that cause me to honor both righteousness and grace. These, it seems to me, are essential elements for building a unity that lasts to eternity. They are perhaps the only things that can overcome our desire to make idols out of ourselves and descend into our worst selves. They may be the only things that can cause us to truly love one another as Jesus loved us and to become truly one.

WHO WE ARE BECOMING

I am known by God and belong to him, as 2 Timothy 2:19 tells me.[1] Belonging to God is an essential part, perhaps the most important part, of my personal identity. It is an unshakeable and reassuring truth about who I am and my relationship to God (Rom. 14:8).

It can also be a central driving force in our lives. Old Testament scholar Carmen Joy Imes states, "What matters most about us is to whom we belong."[2] The significance and power of belonging means this aspect of my identity speaks not just to how I think about myself, but also how I respond to God. The larger point frames the whole. If I belong to him, then my life should reflect that.

It is a truism that we worship what we love. The objects of our worship carry enormous potential to reveal the state of our hearts. Bob Kauflin both encourages and warns us when he says, "What we love most will determine what we genuinely worship."[3] We are called to love our neighbor, but we are first to love God with all our hearts, souls, and minds (Matt. 22:37–39). We must take care not to slip from loving God first to loving justice, or loving being "right," and doing these in the name of loving God.

Maybe the problem is not what we *are* doing as much as what we are *not* doing. We were created to worship. But when God is not the object of our worship, we default into worshiping something else and something lesser. The biggest and most meaningful objects of our affection too often become ourselves and our own thoughts and ideas and fallen desires. When this happens, the inevitable result will be a descent into pride, judgmentalism, blaming, bitterness, and more. We fulfill Romans 1 as we give in to our human nature.

Jesus said that we are to love one another as he has loved us (John 13:34; 15:12), and that this love first comes from the Father (John 15:9; 1 John 4:7–12). As a biblical scholar, my first instinct is to study and analyze. But I am seeing more and more how deceptively easy it is to skip that most critical part of setting my heart and mind to love God. I come away from quiet times and Scripture study with information and principles, but I have not placed my heart before God in devotion, rest, obedience, and awe. The result is I become someone who has knowledge that "puffs up" rather than someone who has love that "builds up" (1 Cor. 8:1). I even become someone whose knowledge leads to great harm because I either don't care or am clueless as to how my actions and pronouncements impact people (1 Cor. 8:9–13).

Perhaps one of the hardest things to do is to admit

that we don't love, that we don't love as we ought, that we don't love what—or who—we are supposed to love. But maybe recognizing these uncomfortable truths about ourselves is not such a bad place to be, for it can compel us to realize that we are all desperately needy and insufficient. Perhaps that is what is necessary for us to come before the throne. This is the beauty we see in the vision of Revelation with its unimaginable picture of a unified church before the almighty, transcendent God in a humility that reflects the Lamb who was slain. Here is an important part of the church's final salvation. It comes from neither our cleverness nor our courage but from our submission to God as we seek what only he can give and as we present our hearts so they might be changed.

Revelation tells me that worship matters, really matters, because it orients my heart to God's bigness so I can accurately see my own smallness and what that means. This posture causes me to trust in God and his Son, Jesus, rather than focusing on my personal frailties. Ironically, it does not obliterate me as an individual nor squelch my individuality. On the contrary, it gives me the proper context for my specific human existence as neither unimportant nor the center. Rather, I matter because I was created by God and belong to him. As someone uniquely formed and given the breath of life by my Creator, I live in a larger world that he has also made and am a member of the body of his Son. This is my fundamental reality.

By the Spirit of Christ, all of us as God's creation are to be unified in heart and mind, sharing the same love and having the same care for each other (Phil. 2:1–4).

The more we come before God around his magnificent, overwhelming, and humbling throne, the more may we come together to proclaim the salvation offered in Christ as a people gathered "from every nation, tribe, people and language" (Rev. 7:9).

In the end, this is who we are . . . and hopefully who we are becoming.

ACKNOWLEDGMENTS

Although I only started writing this book in the last few years, the stories and reflections have been years in the making. I am grateful both to those who had a more direct impact on making this book a reality and to those who encouraged and supported me at critical times in my journey.

I am thankful to Madison Trammel, who was the first to see the potential of the idea and opened the door for me. His interest in the project helped me believe this was an idea that had promise and should be pursued.

It has been a great pleasure to work with the outstanding team at Zondervan. I have learned much from Ryan Pazdur's keen eye as an editor and have very much appreciated his understanding and support for a different kind of voice in the discussion. I am also grateful for the skill of Matthew Estel for polishing the manuscript and smoothing out rough edges and the expertise of Alexis DeWeese in working on the cover and marketing plan.

Every year I see more and more how my childhood friends were and are so important to me. Although I did not use your names, or I changed your names, you know who you are. Thank you for caring for me and making me feel valued during those critical years, as well as for sharing all those band trips, tennis matches, and piano recitals.

As I have gone on in life, I have gained new friends as well, who have contributed to the book in various ways. They have caused me to see things in a new way, helped me find resources, provided constant encouragement, and kept me in prayer throughout this process. Thank you, Joyce Brooks, David Chung, Alicia Dewey, Octavio Esqueda, Laura Holt, David Horner, Howard Hsieh, June Hetzel, Joanne Jung, Daniel Kim, Joy Mosbarger, Betty Talbert, Katie Tuttle, and Thaddeus Williams. You have provided community and enriched my life by exhibiting God's love, acceptance, and wisdom.

My husband, John, has spent years helping me process the thoughts that have found their way into this book. I am ever grateful for his patient and skillful editing, his keen theological sense, and his constant enthusiastic encouragement for my projects. He spent countless hours reading draft after draft, and agonizing with me over the best way to say something. Thank you for sticking with this to the end, and even more for helping me believe that I had something to say.

Thank you to the Andersons, for making my family feel like part of your family, when we felt out of place and alone.

Lastly, thank you, Dad and Mom, for making the courageous decision to come to America and for all you sacrificed so we could have a better life, and to my siblings, for letting me share these parts of our story, for your support for this book, and for fielding my emails as I tried to figure out details of our parents' journey. And most of all, thank you, Marie, for making growing up a lot of fun and opening up the world to me in so many ways.

NOTES

Chapter 1: Beginnings

1. Terry Wardle, *Identity Matters* (Abilene: Leafwood, 2017), 36.
2. Kenneth Berding, *What Are Spiritual Gifts? Rethinking the Conventional View* (Grand Rapids: Kregel: 2006).
3. And which some people argue is more of a part of 1 Corinthians 13 anyway, the great hymn on love.

Chapter 2: Not Fitting In

1. Charles Taylor, *Sources of the Self: The Making of the Modern Identity* (Cambridge: Harvard University Press, 1989), 35.
2. "Naming," *The Baker Illustrated Bible Dictionary*, ed. Tremper Longman III (Grand Rapids: Baker, 2013): 1196–97.
3. Kandy Queen-Sutherland, "Naming," *Holman Bible Dictionary*, ed. Trent C. Butler (Nashville: Holman Bible Publishers, 1991).
4. David A. deSilva, *Honor, Patronage, Kinship & Purity* (Downers Grove: InterVarsity, 2000), 163.
5. "Names of God," *The Baker Illustrated Bible Dictionary*, ed. Tremper Longman III (Grand Rapids: Baker, 2013): 1194–96.

Chapter 3: Rejection and Grace

1. Michelle Lee-Barnewall, *Surprised by the Parables: Growing in Grace through the Stories of Jesus* (Bellingham: Lexham, 2020), 30.

2. Thanks go to Julie Maxham, who brought this to my attention in her thesis, "Witness, Discipleship, and Hospitality: A Lukan Theology of Women in the Ministry of Jesus" (ThM thesis, Talbot School of Theology, 2017), 122.

3. What I was experiencing could have been what has been called the cultural normalization of Whiteness. As Alistair Bonnett describes, "Whiteness has, at least within the modern era and within Western societies, tended to be constructed as a norm, an unchanging and unproblematic location, a position from which all other identities come to be marked by their difference." Bonnett, "White Studies: The Problems and Projects of a New Research Agenda," *Theory, Culture & Society* 13, no. 2 (1996): 146. Hence, my belief that Whiteness was "normal," so I was not. In this, White becomes the "default" or assumed norm against which other things, or people, are measured. Daniel Hill, *White Awake* (Downers Grove, IL: InterVarsity Press, 2017), 31–38.

4. Qian Julie Wang, *Beautiful Country* (New York: Knopf Doubleday, 2021), 82.

5. Carl R. Trueman, *The Rise and Triumph of the Modern Self: Cultural Amnesia, Expressive Individualism, and the Road to the Sexual Revolution* (Wheaton, IL: Crossway, 2020), 57.

Chapter 4: A Part of Something Bigger

1. I also suspect that Paul would not so easily distinguish between individual and corporate identity. However, for our current purposes, it is probably more helpful to talk about them separately here.

2. For a more detailed argument on the ontological nature of the body of Christ and the relationship to Paul's imperatives, see my earlier work, Michelle V. Lee, *Paul, the Stoics, and the Body of Christ*, SNTSMS 137 (Cambridge: Cambridge University Press, 2006).

Chapter 5: The Power of Corporate Identity

1. There are some who do address this. A helpful book in this regard is Jarvis J. Williams, *One New Man* (Nashville: B&H, 2010). Williams looks at racial reconciliation through a broad theological overview of human sin and divine redemption.
2. Bruce Berglund, "The 'Miracle on Ice' Shaped the Olympic Coverage We're Seeing Every Night," *Washington Post*, February 9, 2022, https://www.washingtonpost.com /outlook/2022/02/09/miracle-ice-shaped-olympics -coverage-were-seeing-every-night/.
3. For the Stoics, all humanity existed as a body, which was also the basis of every person's obligation to all humanity. See Lee, *Paul, the Stoics, and the Body of Christ*, 46–58.
4. It did not mean belonging as in "ownership."
5. Or *oikeiosis* in the Greek. Lee, *Paul, the Stoics, and the Body of Christ*, 69–74.
6. I don't recall where I first came across this idea, but since then I have found some articles discussing it, e.g., https:// www.bbc.com/news/science-environment-38920193.

Chapter 6: The Church as a Family

1. For example, Robert Banks, *Paul's Idea of Community*, rev. ed. (Peabody: Hendrickson, 1994), 49.
2. Joseph H. Hellerman, *The Ancient Church as Family: Early Christian Communities and Surrogate Kinship* (Minneapolis: Fortress, 2001), 36.

3. Joseph H. Hellerman, *When the Church Was a Family: Recapturing Jesus' Vision for Authentic Christian Community* (Nashville: B&H Academic, 2009), 16.

4. E.g., Matt. 8:21–22; 10:34–38; 12:46–50; Mark 3:31–35; 8:34–35; Luke 8:19–21; 9:57–62; 12:51–55; 14:25–27.

5. Hellerman, *When the Church Was a Family*, 55.

6. Michael J. Wilkins, *Matthew*, NIVAC (Grand Rapids: Zondervan, 2004), 351.

7. Nijay K. Gupta, *1–2 Thessalonians*, New Covenant Commentary (Eugene, OR: Cascade, 2016), 17.

8. Banks also points out his use of the "warmest" terms about particular individuals, such as Tychicus, who is a "beloved brother" (Col. 4:7; Eph. 6:21 ESV) and Philemon, about whom he says, "I have derived much joy and comfort from your love, my brother" (Philem. 7 ESV). *Paul's Idea of Community*, 51.

9. Gk: ἐν σπλάγχνοις. Gerald F. Hawthorne, *Philippians*, WBC 43 (Waco, TX: Word, 1983), 29.

10. This is reflected in writings such as Sir. 25:1, "I take pleasure in three things, and they are beautiful in the sight of God and of mortals: agreement among brothers and sisters, friendship among neighbors, and a wife and a husband who live in harmony." Hellerman, *When the Church Was a Family*, 64.

11. Hellerman has counted 139 occurrences of the Greek root (*adelph-*) for this sibling terminology in Paul's letters, with most referring to the church family. *When the Church Was a Family*, 77–78.

12. John H. Elliot, "The Jesus Movement Was Not Egalitarian but Family-Oriented," *BibInt* 11 (2003), 177.

13. David E. Garland, *1 Corinthians*, Baker Exegetical Commentary on the New Testament (Grand Rapids: Baker, 2003), 378.

14. Banks, *Paul's Idea of Community*, 51.

15. The relationship between principles, or the law, and life in the Spirit (e.g., the "law of Christ" [Gal. 6:2]) is a well-traveled topic in Pauline studies. In my own research, I examined the way in which Paul used rules or principles as guides for those still progressing in their Christian walk, while teaching the believers that the deepest unity must be founded on the internalization of their corporate identity and identification with the example of Jesus's love, self-sacrifice, and other-centeredness. Lee, *Paul, the Stoics, and the Body of Christ*.

16. We see the juxtaposition of Paul's statements on oneness and his exhortations for love and peace elsewhere in his letters (e.g., Rom. 12:3–13:21; Eph. 2:14–18; Col. 3:12–15).

Chapter 7: Seeing and Being Seen

1. Trueman, *Rise and Triumph of the Modern Self*, 59.
2. Leonard Mlodinow, *Subliminal: How Your Unconscious Mind Rules Your Behavior* (New York: Vintage, 2012), 146.
3. Mlodinow, *Subliminal*, 156. Or as Jennifer L. Eberhardt notes, categorization is not automatically bias, but it can be a "precursor to bias." *Biased: Uncovering the Hidden Prejudice That Shapes What We See, Think, and Do* (New York: Penguin, 2020), 30.
4. Octavio Javier Esqueda, "What's Your Immigration Status? Divine," *Christianity Today*, September 6, 2017, https://www.christianitytoday.com/ct/2017/september -web-only/jesus-divine-immigration-status-daca.html.

Chapter 8: Different by Design

1. Paul says that the "mystery of Christ" is that gentiles as well as Jews are included as sharers in the promises of Christ. The soteriological inclusion of the gentiles into the new covenant community would have profound relational implications for the two enemy groups.

Michelle Lee-Barnewall, *Neither Complementarian nor Egalitarian: A Kingdom Corrective to the Evangelical Gender Debate* (Grand Rapids: Eerdmans, 2016), 86–87.

2. Particularly as related to Colossians 3:11, these new attitudes involve putting off the "old man" related to the worldly culture belonging to the realm of the flesh, and putting on the "new man" in Christ. J. Daniel Hays, *From Every People and Nation: A Biblical Theology of Race*, NSBT (Downers Grove: InterVarsity, 2003), 189.

3. This phrase is used by Amy Chua to describe, for example, the former political situation in the United States in which the American Left and American Right spoke in terms of national unity and transcending group divides, a situation which tragically has disintegrated today. *Political Tribes: Group Instinct and the Fate of Nations* (New York: Penguin, 2018), 178.

4. William S. Campbell, *Paul and the Creation of Christian Identity* (London: T&T Clark, 2008), 54–57.

5. Similarly, the patriarchs are his "fathers" (Acts 26:6; 28:17 ESV).

6. Aaron Kuecker, *The Spirit and the "Other": Social Identity, Ethnicity and Intergroup Reconciliation in Luke-Acts* (New York: T&T Clark, 2011), 221.

7. Harold W. Hoehner, *Ephesians* (Grand Rapids: Baker, 2002), 370.

8. It is remarkable how the New Testament writers do not shy away from showing us various conflicts in the early church, whether between Jews and gentiles, different Jewish factions (Acts 6:1), or even the founding apostles themselves (Acts 15:36–41; Gal. 2:11–21)!

9. Elizabeth Lewis Hall, "What are Bodies for? An Integrative Examination of Embodiment," *Christian Scholar's Review* 39 (2010), 160.

10. Gregg Allison, *Embodied: Living as Whole People in a Fractured World* (Grand Rapids: Baker, 2021), 27.

11. Dallas Willard, *The Spirit of the Disciplines* (San Francisco: HarperSanFrancisco, 1988), 28.

12. Willard, *The Spirit of the Disciplines*, 33.

13. Susan Grove Eastman, *Paul and the Person: Reframing Paul's Anthropology* (Grand Rapids: Eerdmans, 2017), 70.

14. This may reflect what Shaun Gallagher calls, "body-environment-intersubjectivity." Shaun Gallagher, *How the Body Shapes the Mind* (Oxford: Oxford University Press, 2005), 242–43.

15. The Diaspora is the geographical dispersion of the Jews from Israel, especially after the destruction of the temple and the Babylonian exile.

16. It is also likely that they were residents, not visitors. Most would be Diaspora Jews who had settled in Jerusalem, and not just those who were visiting for the festival season. Craig S. Keener, *Acts: An Exegetical Commentary*, vol. 1, *Introduction and 1:1–2:47* (Grand Rapids: Baker, 2012), 833.

17. The thoughts of Kuecker are quite helpful here. *The Spirit and the "Other"*, 111–24.

Chapter 9: Called to Live Together

1. Chua, *Political Tribes*, 1.

2. Gordon D. Fee, "Male and Female in the New Creation. Galatians 3:26–29," *Discovering Biblical Equality*, ed. Ronald W. Pierce and Rebecca Merrill Groothius (Downers Grove, IL: InterVarsity, 2005), 176.

3. Paul K. Jewett, *Man as Male and Female* (Grand Rapids: Eerdmans, 1975), 143.

4. Garland, *1 Corinthians*, 536.

5. Richard A. Horsley, *1 Corinthians*, Abingdon New

Testament Commentaries (Nashville: Abingdon, 1998), 160.

6. Garland, *1 Corinthians*, 541 as seen in sources such as Athenaeus, *Deipnosophistae* 8.365AB.

7. As Lynn H. Cohick notes, the church's unity "should undercut their social hierarchies. The rejection of favoritism helps us understand the type of unity Paul desires—it is not about creating uniformity but about renouncing cultural privilege." *The Letter to the Ephesians*, NICNT (Grand Rapids: Eerdmans, 2020), 182.

8. *Subliminal*, 174.

9. Social scientists would seem to agree with my neighbor's experience and friend's assessment. In his study on racial attitudes in the early twentieth century, Emory S. Bogardus developed a scale, which is still used today, that measured America's ethno-racial hierarchy. In that scale, Swedes came out on top among the Scandinavians, followed by Norwegians, Danes, and then the Finns. *Immigration and Race Attitudes* (Boston: D.C. Heath and Company, 1928), 25.

10. The literature on this seems to have exploded in recent years, particularly as more research has come out on the effects of social media, but a key earlier work seems to be that of Jean M. Twenge and W. Keith Campbell, *The Narcissism Epidemic: Living in the Age of Entitlement* (New York: Atria, 2009).

11. William S. Campbell, "Unity and Diversity in the Church: Transformed Identities and the Peace of Christ in Ephesians," *Transformation* 25 (2008), 15.

Chapter 10: Acknowledging Our Limitations

1. "Peace," *The Westminster Dictionary of Theological Terms*, ed. Donald K. McKim, 2nd ed. (Louisville: Westminster John Knox, 2014), 232.

2. Lynn H. Cohick, *Ephesians,* New Covenant Commentary (Cambridge: Lutterworth, 2010), 74.

3. Ecclesiastes 1:9.

4. Te-Li Lau describes how ancient thinkers such as Aristotle were mindful of the danger of division based on racial distinctions for creating civil instability. *The Politics of Peace: Ephesians, Dio Chrysostom, and the Confucian Four Books,* NovTSup 133 (Leiden: Brill, 2010), 81–82.

5. For some helpful summaries of this topic, see Richard L. Rohrbaugh, "Honor: Core Value in the Biblical World," in *Understanding the Social World of the New Testament,* ed. Dietmar Neufeld and Richard E. DeMaris (New York: Routledge, 2010), 109–25; Joseph H. Hellerman, *Reconstructing Honor in Roman Philippi: Carmen Christi as Cursus Pudorum,* SNTSMS 132 (Cambridge: Cambridge University Press, 2005), 3–33; deSilva, *Honor,* 42.

6. We can note other places where Paul is not averse to hierarchy, and actually sees it as fundamental to the community, as he elsewhere seems to rank the gifts (e.g., 1 Cor. 12:28) or proclaim some as worthy of more honor (1 Tim. 5:17–18).

7. For a more detailed description of the Greco-Roman philosophical background, see the insightful work of Dale Martin, *The Corinthian Body* (New Haven, CT: Yale University Press, 1995), 88–92; "Tongues of Angels and Other Status Indicators," *Journal of the American Academy of Religion* 59 (1991): 547–89.

8. We further see the implications of the irony in the expected hierarchy of the Spirit (*pneuma*) and the mind (*nous*), especially in regard to which agent controls the person. Paul sees the superiority of prophecy in its use of both the spirit and the mind (1 Cor. 14:15–16). Tongues engages only the spirit (1 Cor. 14:14). Martin argues that the *pneuma* was viewed as being superior to the

nous. This is a Platonic hierarchy which also appears in Philo. Therefore, when Paul says in 1 Cor. 14 that the *nous* and the *pneuma* should work together in producing manifestations that will build up the community, this implies a reversal of status. "Paul's insistence on an equal partnership of the higher- and lower-status entities would have been heard as a reversal of their statuses. To say that the *pneuma* should give up its claim to rule unchallenged when it comes upon the scene— that it should join the *nous* in a mutually cooperative agreement—is to imply a lowering of the status of the *pneuma* to the level of or below the *nous*" (Martin, *Corinthian Body*, 96–102).

9. David Lamb, "Massachusetts Mill Town Gets Christmas Angel for Christmas," *Los Angeles Times*, December 19, 1995, https://www.latimes.com/archives/la-xpm-1995-12 -19-mn-15648-story.html.

10. Shelley Donald Coolidge, "'Corporate Decency' Prevails at Malden Mills," *Christian Science Monitor*, March 28, 1996, https://www.csmonitor.com/1996/0328/28015.html.

11. Daniel B. Green, "This Day in Jewish History: 1995: Malden Mills Burns Down, Shows What an Employer with a Heart Looks Like," *Haaretz*, December 11, 2015, https://www.haaretz.com/jewish/.premium-1995 -malden-mills-burns-down-1.5435757.

12. Not everyone agrees with this analysis, although it seems to have been the dominant conclusion in the business community. In one article, the author proposes that three warmer than usual winters contributed to lower sales of the cold weather products, not just Feuerstein's generosity. David W. Gill, "Was Aaron Feuerstein Wrong?" *Ethix*, June 25, 2011, https://ethix .org/2011/06/25/was-aaron-feuerstein-wrong.

13. Lynnley Browning, "Management; Fire Could Not Stop

a Mill, but Debts May," *New York Times*, November 28, 2001; https://www.nytimes.com/2001/11/28/business /management-fire-could-not-stop-a-mill-but-debts-may .html.

14. Rabbi Avi Shafran, "Aaron Feuerstein: Bankrupt and Wealthy," Aish, June 29, 2002, https://www.aish.com/ci /be/48881397.html.

Chapter 11: When Everyone Is Wrong

1. This is provided, of course, that it is not a matter of core doctrine. Of these, Paul is quite clear, for example, in the case of Hymenaeus and Alexander, whom he considers to be blasphemers and so expelled from the church (1 Tim. 1:18–20). But Paul actually sees several grey areas, sometimes referred to as *adiaphora*, in which the larger issue is how to unify a divided church.

2. This seems to be the majority view of New Testament commentators. For a brief overview of other proposed views, you can see the essay in Colin G. Kruse, *Paul's Letter to the Romans*, PNTC (Grand Rapids: Eerdmans, 2012), 509–10.

3. Paul refers to the groups as the weak and the strong (e.g., Rom. 15:1, etc.). It is important to keep in mind that Paul considers both groups to be full members of the community. The question of saving faith is not in view. Instead, *weak* may refer to being "troubled in conscience," for those who did not fully grasp the implications of the gospel and so whose consciences did not allow them to do some things even though they were now permitted as believers in Christ (Kruse, *Romans*, 511). They may be abstaining from meat to maintain Old Testament purity laws due to the difficulty of getting kosher meat in their pagan context. The question over the nature of certain days could also have its origin

in the Old Testament law, particularly in Sabbath observance. The gentile Christians, however, would not have the same purity concerns (Douglas J. Moo, *The Letter to the Romans*, NICNT [Grand Rapids: Eerdmans, 2018], 837). Furthermore, *weak* is likely a title imposed upon the members by the more dominant "strong" group. In other words, it is not necessarily Paul's characterization of the group (Robert Jewett, *Romans*, Hermeneia [Minneapolis: Fortress, 2006], 834–35). In this chapter I will avoid referring to the groups as strong and weak to avoid possible mischaracterizations or misleading implications. For example, while the strong correspond to the more progressive view, it is not always the case that Paul would consider the more traditional view to be weak.

4. I am working from the premise that the issue of food here is what is often called a "grey area," in other words, an area in which Scripture does not specifically state how a believer should act.

5. Donald K. McKim, ed., "Peace," *The Westminster Dictionary of Theological Terms*, 2nd ed. (Louisville: Westminster John Knox, 2014), 232.

Chapter 12: Knowing Our Place

1. Attributed to Louise Bush-Brown, reported as unverified in *Respectfully Quoted: A Dictionary of Quotations* (Washington, DC: Library of Congress, 1989).

2. As J. Scott Duvall states, Jesus has "purchased" a "multicultural people" by his sacrifice. Duvall, *Revelation*, Teach the Text Commentary Series (Grand Rapids: Baker, 2014), 95.

3. When Paul talks about doing the "same things," he does not necessarily mean the precisely same actions, but more likely the same sins of the heart in Romans

1:29–31, such as pride, arrogance, and maligning. Moo, *Romans*, 141.

4. Biographer Ellen Vaughn notes that although the tribe was referred to as the "Auca" by the missionaries and others during that time, the tribe's actual name is the Waodani. "Auca" is now understood to be a slur, although it was certainly not used or understood in that way by the missionaries. Vaughn, *Becoming Elisabeth Elliot* (Nashville: B&H, 2020), 5–7.

5. Elisabeth Elliot, *Through Gates of Splendor* (Wheaton: Tyndale, 1988), 18.

6. As John N. Oswalt notes, the sequence is critical: "The vision of God leads to self-despair, self-despair opens the door to cleansing; cleansing makes it possible to recognize the possibility of service; the total experience then leads to an offering of oneself." Oswalt, *The Book of Isaiah: Chapters 1–39*, NICOT (Grand Rapids: Eerdmans, 1986), 186.

Chapter 13: In Awe

1. Paul Piff and Daphne Keltner, "Why Do We Experience Awe?," *New York Times*, May 22, 2015, https://www .nytimes.com/2015/05/24/opinion/sunday/why-do-we -experience-awe.html.

2. Piff and Keltner, "Why Do We Experience Awe?"

3. Interestingly, the movie portrays the end of the fighting as being the result of a transcendent goal that caused the two factions to look beyond themselves: saving the life of Gandhi, who pledged to fast until the fighting stopped.

4. One thing to observe here is the connection with the account of the beginning of the world in Genesis. As Hays describes, Genesis 10–11 describes the scattering of the nations because of their rebellion. They were diversified into many languages and nations under his

wrath. The unity of God's people in Revelation of "every tribe and language and people and nation" (Rev. 5:9; 7:9; 11:9; 14:6) connects with the promise to Abraham in Gen. 12:1–3 to bless all the "nations" through him. Hays, *From Every People and Nation*, 60–62, 165, 193–99.

5. As Darrell L. Bock explains, "This honouring of God serves as an introduction, an overture, to the entire letter. Reconciliation is at the base of the church. Such reconciliation reflects a way of life that is distinctive about Christians. It is a crucial goal in salvation. It stands prominent among the array of blessings that are rooted in the salvation that comes in Christ. So in the body of the letter Paul will turn from what salvation gives to what it means for our walk and identity. The fact that the church, reconciliation and the distinctive ways of living are not mentioned here at the start does not disqualify the note of praise from setting up such themes, acting as the theological base for the development Paul will present." *Ephesians: An Introduction and Commentary*, Tyndale New Testament Commentaries (Downers Grove, IL: InterVarsity, 2019), 32.

6. A main point of the throne room scene is the salvation brought about by Christ's sacrifice. The Lamb is worthy to take the scroll because he "purchased" people for God by his death (5:9). So while Jesus as the Lion of the tribe of Judah is initially proclaimed as worthy to open the scroll (5:5), after this declaration John sees not a lion but a lamb (5:6). The emphasis is that it is as the Lamb that Jesus is worshiped by his people here. The declaration of worship of God and the Lamb in chapter 7 makes no mention of the Lion of the tribe of Judah. As Richard Bauckham states, Revelation shows how "God is related to the world not only as the transcendent holy One, but also as the slaughtered Lamb." *The Theology of the Book*

of Revelation (Cambridge: Cambridge University Press, 1993), 65.

7. Although Jesus is identified as the Lion of the tribe of Judah as the one worthy to open the scroll, when John actually sees Jesus, he sees the Lamb, and it is as the Lamb that Christ is worshiped (Rev. 5:5–8). It is the appearance of the Lamb instead the Lion that is the point. As Ian Paul describes, "The powerful figure of a lion is in stark contrast to the vulnerability of the lamb." Paul, *Revelation*, TNTC (Downers Grove, IL: IVP Academic, 2018), 132. Or perhaps as Gordon D. Fee states, "The only lion in heaven is in fact the Slain Lamb." Fee further notes that even though Revelation is "interested above all in God's justice, no lion ever appears in heaven." However, the Lamb appears throughout, including at the end, where we find another reference to the Lamb at the throne (22:1–5). Fee, *Revelation: A New Covenant Commentary* (Cambridge: Lutterworth, 2013). 80.

8. Paul, *Revelation*, 132.

9. Bauckham notes that in Jewish monotheism, worship marked "the distinction between the one God the Creator of all things, who must be worshipped, and his creatures, to worship whom is idolatry." *Revelation*, 58.

10. Roof also said he originally thought about killing drug dealers, but decided against it because he thought they would shoot back. "Dylan Roof's Confession, Journal Details Racist Motivation for Killings," *Chicago Tribune*, December 10, 2016, http://www.chicagotribune.com /news/nationworld/ct-dylann-roof-charleston-shooting -20161209-story.html.

11. Sari Horwitz, Chico Harlan, Peter Holley, and William Wan, "What We Know so Far about Charleston Church Shooting Suspect Dylann Roof," *Washington Post*,

June 20, 2015, https://www.washingtonpost.com/news
/post-nation/wp/2015/06/20/what-we-know-so-far
-about-charleston-church-shooting-suspect-dylann-roof/.

12. Nadine Collier, whose mother was one of the victims,
    told Roof, "I forgive you. You took something very
    precious away from me. I will never get to talk to her ever
    again. I will never be able to hold her again, but I forgive
    you. And have mercy on your soul." Mark Berman, "'I
    Forgive You.' Relatives of Charleston Church Shooting
    Victims Address Dylann Roof," *Washington Post*, July 19,
    2015, https://www.washingtonpost.com/news/post
    -nation/wp/2015/06/19/i-forgive-you-relatives-of
    -charleston-church-victims-address-dylann-roof/?utm
    _term=.52540db7d58e.

13. Emily Shapiro, "Charleston Victim's Mother Tells Dylann
    Roof, 'I Forgive You,'" KCRG ABC News, January 11,
    2017, https://www.kcrg.com/content/news/Charleston
    -Victims-Mother-Tells-Dylann-Roof-I-Forgive-You
    -410421885.html.

Conclusion: Who We Are Becoming

1. Brian S. Rosner says that these two concepts are
   essentially "equivalent" here. *Known by God: A Biblical
   Theology of Personal Identity* (Grand Rapids: Zondervan,
   2017), 117.

2. Carmen Joy Imes, *Bearing God's Name: Why Sinai Still
   Matters* (Downers Grove, IL: IVP Academic, 2019), 79.

3. Kauflin, *Worship Matters: Leading Others to Encounter the
   Greatness of God* (Wheaton, IL: Crossway, 2008), 25.